"This book is full of inspiring stories from incredible women who have 'been there and done that.'" —Megan Ferda, MA, LPC

"A thoughtful & insightful book that reveals the challenges, perspectives and realities of today's women." —Dr. Morven R. Baker, PCC-S, NCC, Ashland Women's Counseling Center, Ashland, Ohio

"An anthology of poignant reflections of the struggles and triumphs of a group of women, each describing their individual journeys of self discovery. The women share their definitions of what it means to be a woman and the myriad cultural and personal influences which helped to mold their lives. The word resiliency resonates throughout the stories." —Patricia M. Pakan, Ph.D., R.N. N.B.C.C.

Ordinary Beginnings, Extraordinary Destinations

ISBN: 978-1-60920-094-7
Printed in the United States of America
©2014 Stacey Schneider and Lori Bodkin
All rights reserved

API
Ajoyin Publishing, Inc.
P.O. 342
Three Rivers, MI 49093
www.ajoyin.com

No part of this book may be reproduced or transmitted in any form or by any means, electronic or mechanical—including photocopying, recording, or by any information storage and retrieval system—without permission in writing from the publisher, except as provided by United States of America copyright law.

Please direct your inquiries to admin@ajoyin.com

Contents

- vii   Acknowledgements
- ix   Prologue . . . Ordinary Beginnings.

Section 1

- 2   Story 1 by Kim Smyth
- 6   Story 2 by Anonymous Author
- 11   Story 3 by Alicia Lynch
- 14   Story 4 by Paula Politis
- 17   Story 5 by Hannah Cross
- 20   Story 6 by Ashley Franks
- 24   Story 7 by Kelly Dillon
- 28   Story 8 by Danielle Heideman
- 30   Story 9 by Anonymous Author
- 35   Story 10 by Anonymous Author
- 41   Story 11 by Preet Bajwa
- 43   Story 12 by Anonymous Author
- 45   Story 13 by Anonymous Author
- 48   Story 14 by Chennel Hill
- 50   Story 15 by Anonymous Author
- 53   Story 16 by Megan Elavsky

Section 2

- 61 The Hallmarks of a Woman by Jackie Kruse
- 64 What's Wrong with Women's Rights? by Anonymous Author
- 70 Attitude of Gratitude by Kelly Faiola
- 73 Love After All by Anonymous Author
- 76 From Bullied to Bold by Cindy Coe
- 80 Hiding by Anonymous Author
- 83 Joy in the Journey by Jan L'Ecuyer
- 86 Choices by Amy Zehnder
- 89 Moving Forward by Anonymous Author
- 92 Daddy's Little Girl by Michelle Cudnik
- 96 Thank You, Cancer! by Susan Bruce
- 100 When Life Does Not Go According to Plan by Julia Lawson
- 105 My "Wee Pea" by M. Petrea Cober
- 112 Life's Trials Build Character by Nora Helscel
- 116 When Your Life Hits a Brick Wall by Stacey Schneider
- 121 Who Am I, Really? by Lori Bodkin

- 125 Epilogue ... Extraordinary Destinations
- 127 Questions for Discussion
- 129 About the Authors

Acknowledgements

We are grateful to the many people who believed in our ideas and gave so much of themselves to make the publication of *Ordinary Beginnings, Extraordinary Destinations* possible. There were countless encouragements from friends, family members, and peers to help us along this journey. The women who gave so much of themselves and opened their hearts to share their stories will always hold a special place in our hearts. Thank you to all of those who edited and got us to the final round. We are grateful for your tireless hours of work and listening ears. A very special thank you to Natalie Zambori for creating and painting our beautiful cover design. Most of all, the co-editors would like to thank each other and God for knowing when to put two people together who were on the same track, but both needed a nudge in the right direction with a little boost of confidence and unfailing love and support.

Prologue... Ordinary Beginnings

As I sat down to write an introduction for this book, it took me back to that small little classroom with a handful of remarkable women who sat around a table discussing what it was like to be a female. As I sat there and looked at each and every one of them, who I had come to know and love throughout the three years I was their teacher, I realized they were so different but yet oh so similar. They came from different families, had different backgrounds, different experiences, different skin colors but one thing bonded us... we were women. Through that single thread, I began to see so many similarities in each of our stories. We alone thought we had to be perfect and carry the weight of the world. We alone had to fulfill everyone's desires but our own. We alone had to live up to that myth of the superwoman who could do it all. We were determined to have a successful career, a doting husband, two beautiful children, a golden retriever, a house with a white picket fence and balance all of this while remaining ageless with the body of a twenty year old. What would happen when we couldn't keep all the balls in the air? Well, we would label our lives as failures, of course. I came from the generation where I was taught if you wanted something and worked hard enough you would be able to attain it. Sitting around the room that afternoon, I realized we all had something remarkable to share with the world. We had stories of how we became the superwomen we were really meant to be. Not the ideal we had all built up in our head, but the women we would grow into and come to love in our own time.

So, here are the stories of some of those remarkable women. Lori and I wanted to give you a peek into their lives, to let you know that you are not alone on this journey called life; that there are women out there who are just like you. Reach out and find a friend who will support you and love you. She too has most likely walked a mile in your shoes.

You will find this book has two different sections. The first section is written by our younger writers. They have just begun their journey in discovering who they are, but yet you will see so many remarkable stories. The second section is written by our experienced women. They have made many journeys already. You will see the amazing women they have become and discover the lessons they have learned. You will love them for the fabulous women they are today and you will love our younger writers for the fabulous women they are about to become. Each one of these women started with an ordinary beginning and is well on her way to her own extraordinary destination. So grab a comfortable spot (and maybe a few tissues) and get ready to meet some dynamic gals!

Stacey

Section 1

Hi. *My name is Kim and I have long hair.* Well, sometimes I have long hair but other times I have short hair because I like to give mine to people who need it.

You see, I am a firm believer that confidence can make or break a woman. For some reason we, as females, are programmed to constantly compare ourselves to those around us. "Am I as pretty as her?" "She seems so much smarter than me." All sorts of questions and judgments go through our heads each and every day causing us to second guess what a good person we are and how valuable we can be. Some of us will never outgrow these thoughts and will continue to be uncomfortable with who we are as a person, but others will blossom and become fabulous, confident women.

When I was growing up, I struggled with all the negative thoughts in my head. I always tried to hide my insecurities with my physical appearance. I think many of us do. Why else would we dye our hair, paint our faces, and wear uncomfortable clothes and shoes that bind us all day long? Inside I knew that I was a good person, but I didn't know if I was as good of a person as the girl sitting next to me. For years I battled with confidence and my outward appearance served as my safety blanket. I started to grow out of this phase as I got older. At some point in high school I confided in my best friends about how I always felt inadequate because I was constantly comparing myself to them. I was surprised to find that they had been doing the same thing and felt inferior to me. This set our brains on a whirlwind that ended with us concluding all females must feel some sort of self-doubt or inferiority while growing up.

It is a shame that a female has to second guess herself. We are all lovely, unique, wonderful human beings that have something magnificent to offer this world. Unfortunately our insecurities usually get the better of us and we find ourselves hiding instead of showing everyone how great we are. I came to this conclusion in high school, and I wanted to do everything I could to make sure no girl had to hide her inner beauty because of some silly insecurities. With this in mind, my friends and I began talking about how we could best help those who were lacking confidence. We came to the unanimous conclusion that we would donate our hair. To a female, hair is much more than a part of the body. It is what we use to cover up blemishes and distract others from our uncertainty. It is our safety blanket. I don't know what I would have done without my hair through all of those uncomfortable years. It made me wonder how young girls who aren't able to grow their own hair felt. It seemed like an easy decision. I was able to grow hair. I wasn't really doing anything with it. I had more than enough to donate. So why should I be so selfish and keep this thing that I didn't need? All I could think was, "I could give someone a little peace of mind and one less thing to worry about." Right before graduation I went with my two best friends and cut my hair. I packaged it up and mailed it away to a company who makes wigs. It was so rewarding! It is an incredible feeling knowing that you are able to give someone a little extra confidence with something that you yourself don't really need.

Confidence is what gives a woman the ability to be comfortable in her own skin, to go out and challenge the world, and to be happy. It is a wonderful thing to give a woman a little more confidence and to help her realize her self-worth. Every woman should know how important she is, and by giving a piece of myself to another female, I not only helped her blossom, but I also bloomed into a confident woman.

Kim Smyth

I have had many adult influences in my life growing up. I believe the saying is, "It takes an army." My mother was seventeen years old when she gave birth to me and my father was almost nineteen. He decided to live his life elsewhere without keeping in contact with me. I did not meet my father until I was fourteen years old. My mother and grandparents raised me for the majority of my young life. I was lucky to have close friendships with three slightly older and extremely protective male cousins. If you asked me, I would have told you I was one of the boys. Very much the tomboy, I played with more trucks and G.I. Joes than I could count, made sure I tagged along on every outdoor adventure with my cousins that I could, and helped my grandfather with all of the outside chores. I especially liked spying on him while he fixed cars and cursed like there was no tomorrow. I would giggle and think he was the coolest guy in the world. One would translate these characteristics into the traditional gender roles of a boy and yet, I was still a little girl.

My female influences growing up included my mother, grandmother, and aunt—all with very different personalities and life experiences. My mother was adopted and grew into a woman who was very insecure and looks to religion to guide her path. My grandmother was a woman who treated me like her daughter, yet I grew up knowing there were undertones of anger seeded deep inside of her from her own life experiences. My aunt was a strong woman, the mother of three boys, and the primary parent to them. I looked up to her but she scared the crap out of me at times! My grandfather played the dominant male role in my life—stoic, kind, and the most generous man you will ever meet. My father was a motivated and determined individual. All of these people contributed to the woman I am today.

So what does it mean to be a girl, a woman? Is there *one* true definition? Absolutely not. Of course, we can place those oh-so-comfortable gender roles on our children and ourselves and expect these roles to be fulfilled, but what happens when they aren't? What happens when our children stray from our ideals, values, or expectations? My answer is who cares? Isn't the more important question, "Are they confident, kind, and empathetic individuals?"

I can say the woman that I am today is not who I would have predicted while I was growing up. As a little girl, I thought I would one day grow up, go to college, meet the man I would marry and we would have two kids and two dogs and live in a nice house … blah, blah, blah. Well, my path was a little different than that. I dated but never "fit" with someone. I came close with one man, but I ended it because the love faded, at least on my end. I eventually realized why there was never that "fit." Turns out, I'm a lesbian. I won't go into the details of how I discovered this about myself but there was no denying this was the piece of myself I was missing or simply didn't allow myself to explore before the age of nineteen. Well, that made me question a lot of things like … Who am I? Why didn't I know this about myself? Does this make me any less of a woman? How will my family respond? How will I navigate society and its discrimination? How will I marry someone I love when the laws don't allow it? How will I have children? So many questions and no one to give me the answers. Over the past ten years, I've grown into a person I am proud to be. I have taken qualities from those major influential people and used them to navigate life. I found out all on my own the answers to those questions I asked myself and I want to share them with you.

Who am I? I have grown into a woman who is determined, motivated, dependable, caring, and generous. I hold honesty and respect as two of my most important values. I love with everything inside of me and making others laugh is a top priority.

Why didn't I know this about myself? I grew up thinking being gay was wrong. I never allowed myself to even consider this could be a way of life for me. I was taught that people who are gay go to Hell or are sinners. Well, that's just a bunch of malarkey! I realize now, love is not a sin.

Does this make me any less of a woman? No way, I am very much still a woman! Being a woman is not defined as being with a man, is it? Because if it is, we just set ourselves back fifty years, ladies.

How will my family respond? I found that out right away! And the answer was, not well. My mother informed me I would be going to Hell (surprise, surprise). My father was less than thrilled and slightly confused. His first thoughts were, "If I could give you some of my hormones, then maybe you wouldn't be gay." He was implying that he is a "horndog" and loves women. Clearly, he was confused because I DO love women and "hormones" have nothing to do with it. I can now say, after ten years (eight and a half of those years in one relationship), most of my family has accepted my sexual orientation. It sure was not easy for the first ten years though.

How will I navigate society and its discrimination? I have found out that this is the toughest of all the questions and it is a continuous struggle. I continue to dodge the "Do you have a boyfriend?" or "What does your husband do?" question. I worry that if I tell people at work I am gay and I have a wife, I could jeopardize my career. I still tell people ... I'm just careful with whom I tell. I am truly torn between the concepts of "coming completely out of the closet" or just telling those with whom I feel comfortable. Like I said, this is a continuous struggle.

How will I marry someone I love when the laws don't allow it? Screw the laws, I still got married! My wife and I went to Toronto, Ontario, where she is from, and exchanged vows in front of three witnesses and an officiate. When we returned, we had a "faux ceremony and reception" for our friends and family to celebrate with us. I say faux because the state I am from does not allow same-sex marriage. The gay climate is changing though and rights are on the way!

How will I have children? Clearly, I was confused with how babies are made when I asked myself this question! Duh, young me, sperm banks! One of the best things about being a married lesbian is you have TWO uteruses in the family! Split up the work! The truth is, my spouse and I have already made plans to start a family and let's just say, it is not that far in the future.

As you can see, not much has stopped me from accomplishing my dreams; I just took a different path to get there. I am a strong, determined, and caring woman that has an amazing support system in my spouse. The influences I had in my life growing up molded me into the person I am today and I am proud of the woman I have become.

Anonymous Author

Growing up, I never really felt this great distinction of being a female. Maybe that is because I was a little bit of a tomboy and, in some aspects, still am. When I wanted to play football with the neighborhood boys, I just did it and never second-guessed whether or not I should or could do it because I was a girl. Of course, I enjoy some quintessentially "female" activities and identify with female traits. But I have always identified with a lot of stereotypical "male" traits, as well.

Even now, those typical gender roles are so apparent to me in my relationship with my fiancé, Matt. People just assume that a man does certain jobs and a woman does other jobs. That is somewhat true in our relationship in that he does most of the yard work and takes out the trash and I'm responsible for most of the "scrubbing" jobs, like the bathroom and kitchen. But in other ways, we're completely the opposite. He does the majority of the laundry and dishes, while I'm usually the one who assembles furniture and does the "construction" jobs, like installing a tile backsplash and refinishing our kitchen cabinets. Since he was raised with all sisters and no brothers, he is very comfortable with discussing feminine things and engaging in typical female activities, like shopping and gossiping. He is also better at expressing his emotions, which is probably partially due to his extraversion versus my introversion.

I think there is this view in our culture that women are inherently the more empathetic sex; because of that, I have always felt a little left out or different. It has always been difficult for me to identify with or understand other people's emotions. In fact, I usually feel very uncomfortable interacting with someone who is in an emotional state. I finally think I may have identified a possible cause for this. My mother raised me and my two oldest siblings on her own for several years and, as a result, didn't spend a whole lot of time with us. She had to work a day job, night job, and weekend job to support us. In trying to take care of our physical needs, I think she neglected our emotional needs and understandably so. To this day I find it difficult to connect with my patients when they exhibit emotional responses. It continues to make me uncomfortable but I feel I have come a long way since my first encounters with patients. I have worked hard and will continue to work hard to try and understand my patients better.

I actually find it interesting to look at the differences between me and my two oldest siblings versus my two youngest siblings, who were raised by my mom and stepdad (their father). My stepdad has been present for a large majority of my life and I view him as my father, but I think the scars from my non-existent father and emotionally unavailable mother never quite healed. We have never been a family that expresses emotions readily. Of course, I love my parents and I know that they love me, but we have just never been the type to say "I love you", hug and kiss, etc. My younger siblings are very emotionally expressive and have very close relationships with my parents that are very different from my relationship with my parents. My oldest siblings and I have a very unique relationship because we feel this unity that comes from going through so much together when we were young. It's not something that is openly stated but it's something that we know and feel from our past experiences.

My younger siblings will never know what it was like to come from a broken home raised by a single mother. I am grateful that they never have to experience those difficulties.

Of all my siblings, my older sister (who is sixteen months older than me) and I are the closest. I feel like she gives me a lot of my confidence. Whenever I'm with her, I feel like I can do anything and when I'm not feeling great, she's the one I need to call. I feel so blessed to have someone that I can go to for just about anything. Sometimes I actually feel bad for people that haven't had the opportunity to experience a relationship with a sibling as I have. I've loved my relationship with my sister so much that I am considering having more children than I originally planned so that my children have the chance to have those sibling relationships.

I feel all of my life experiences make me who I am today and I can't change the past. I can only look to making myself the best "me" that I can be for my future. I am a female and if I happen to lack some "normal" female personality traits, then so be it. I'm still going to wear my high heels all day then kick them off so I can throw a football with the boys. We are all a product of our past experiences and, while I believe in self-improvement, I think we should all stop trying to be who we think other people want us to be. I will continue to be who I am, with some minor improvements.

Alicia Lynch

Every year my family and I would spend the summer on Amorgos, a small island of Greece in the Aegean Sea. My father was born and raised there, and eventually came to Youngstown, Ohio as an eager internal medicine resident. It was at Northside Hospital where he won the heart of my mother, a nurse at the time. They eventually got married, had a son, and two years later a daughter—me! Looking back now, I realize what a truly blessed childhood I had. As I mentioned before, our summers were spent in Greece. My father's mother, my YiaYia, lived in Greece, as do my uncle, aunt, and two cousins. Not to be forgotten is my extremely large extended family over there. My YiaYia was one of twelve children so I have many, many distant cousins, kind of like *My Big Fat Greek Wedding*. The days were spent skin diving in the Aegean Sea with my father, brother, and cousin, watching them catch our dinner that I would later help prepare with my YiaYia. I was never allowed to handle the harpoon! I was too young and too clumsy. But I would always follow close behind my Dad, kicking my fins as fast as I could so I wouldn't miss a thing. Once, I fell a little behind the group and came face to face with an eel. I learned my lesson and made sure not to stray ever again. I felt safe swimming in my dad's path.

I was by every means a "Daddy's Girl." Even when we would play board games or sports, I was on Dad's team, and my brother was on my mother's team. He taught me to love to read, even buying *Harry Potter and the Sorcerer's Stone* for me in 1999. "I heard this is going to be a very popular book," he said, "and I thought this would be a great one to read together." He often read to my brother and I, even when we got older. He taught me to appreciate good music. I grew up listening to The Beatles, Queen, and Pink Floyd, and I still do to this day. Most importantly, my dad taught me the importance of helping others, and ultimately, he is the reason why I decided to go into healthcare.

My dad was a pulmonologist in Youngstown, the chief of medicine at forum health, and faculty here at the university. He gave me my first "job," cutting and copying recent medical journal articles and filing them for him to read. He definitely stayed on top of medicine this way. He also had really wonderful relationships with his patients. Sadly, I didn't realize how true this statement was until after he was gone.

In 2005, I started my first year of undergraduate schooling. I was bitter that I was stuck at home attending Youngstown State University while all of my friends moved away to different cities. I remember my mom telling me "It's alright, Paula. Everything happens for a reason". She was right. The end of my freshman year, my father was diagnosed with cancer. By the fall of my sophomore year, he had passed. I am so thankful I was living at home, spending my free time with him, whether it would be sitting around playing cards or staying with him during his chemotherapy sessions. I firmly believe that God kept me home for a reason, to be with my father and to support my mother during this hard time.

Fast-forward to calling hours and his funeral—a time that was so blurry and so unreal. So many of his patients attended both, some barely able to walk, some wheeling in oxygen tanks, and some just relatives of a patient he had. I can't tell you the number of times I heard something like "your father saved my life," or "your dad was so kind to my mother". I know people often say words of comfort to a grieving family in such situations, but I believed them. Recently, I was at a site visit and a technician asked me if I was related to Dr. Politis. I said yes, and she proceeded to tell me what a great man he was. It is small things like this that make me want to be more like him.

Today I still try to follow in my father's path. I think about him and pray to him every day. I still try to keep up with his little traditions. I am attempting to grow his award winning dahlias that he took so much pride in this year, but we'll see how that turns out. I went to Greece for the first time in ten years this past summer and went skin diving with my cousin, though I still was not allowed to use the harpoon. I treat others and patients like he would want me to treat them. If he was still around, I like to imagine that we'd grab lunch in a cafe when he would teach, discuss medications, journal articles, politics, movies, etc. There is so much that I have learned and done in school that I would love to tell him about. Though he is not physically here, I'd like to believe he is around me and my family and is proud of what we've accomplished, and I hope to one day be half the healthcare professional he was.

Paula Politis

"I love my father as the stars—he's a bright shining example and a happy twinkling in my heart." —Terri Guillemets

To me *there is nothing special about the way I grew up.* Just a simple girl with a little sister I did everything with. I could never count how many times we were asked if we were twins even though there is a two year difference in age between us. We were pretty inseparable from the get go. We wore matching clothes; we had all the same friends, we both adored horses. There really isn't much more needed to have an instant connection with someone at that age.

As we got older of course there were things that we didn't agree on. What clothes were mine and which were hers, who got to ride shot gun in the car (logically I think it was my prerogative since I was the oldest), and even how to go about certain things with the horses. I loved my sister through it all. There is a story told around my house that when my little sister Heather was born I was so mad at her I wouldn't talk to my mom for three whole days. I was only two! Now I have seen videos of myself when I was younger, and I don't believe for one minute that I was able to not talk to my mom for three whole days but they say it was so.

Apparently when I wanted anything I would seek my dad out to ask him ever so kindly to get me what I wanted. Maybe this is the start of me being a daddy's girl, hmm ... I wonder? One of the things that my sister and I did not do together was work in the garage. I was always outside with my dad fetching him tools and tightening a screw here and a bolt there for him. It made me feel very accomplished that when he asked for a tool I knew exactly where it was at and could save him time finishing his projects. Heather never really cared about being out in the garage. She tried to stand out there with us a few times, but got bored very quickly and went inside. I couldn't imagine how being inside making dinner was that much more exciting than getting to see how things came apart and went back together. I just loved when my dad would show me how something worked from the inside. It's comparable to sitting in physiology class for the first time and seeing how the nephron works, or figuring out a diagram of the nodes of Ranvier on a neuron. Something about the mechanics of things gets me excited.

So I became the son my dad never had, and my sister became an awesome cook like my mom. I have to laugh looking at the pictures if us from back then because I was such a tomboy and she was such a prissy girl who knows how we ever got along? I am always in some kind of sports clothes or car outfits with a baseball cap on backwards. Heather was in whatever was fashionable at the time, even at 6 years old. One other indication that I was not quite like my sister was my NEED to get a Jeep when I grew up. Oh I wanted a Jeep more than anything. My sister and I fantasized about the day I would get my driver's license and we could shop whenever we wanted. You see, I come from a long line of farmers, and we grew up in a very rural part of the county. Although we only have a measly five acres to roam on, my grandparents next door have 100 acres and the neighbors on the other side have thirty and across the street is another twenty-five acres. It was awesome when we wanted to ride our four-wheelers or go shooting our BB guns, but it was not so fun when we wanted to go somewhere. It is a guaranteed thirty minute drive to anywhere fun from my house. We talked of taking the top off the Jeep, picking up friends and spending hours at the mall. When I finally got my Jeep it was everything I expected and more. I loved that thing despite the holes in the floor I used to lose things out of, or the rain coming down the inside of the windshield that eventually ran down the dashboard and shorted out my gas gauge and sometimes the radio. It was an underpowered rust bucket on wheels, but it was mine and it was our freedom.

When we weren't in the jeep driving around we were on the horses or at the barn prepping for fair. It's the one thing we looked forward to every year. We worked our tails off all year to bring a good horse to the fair. We got to enjoy it in all its glory for one week (and sadly not even a full week since it runs from Tuesday to Sunday) then it is gone. Soon we start prepping for fair next year all over again. Oh the simple life of a country girl. That brings me to the sad part of my story where my sister marries the man she loves. Which shouldn't be so sad, but he took her from me and moved her to Mississippi. Even at my wedding where she was the matron of honor I only got to see her for two days and one doesn't count since it was my wedding day. It is hard learning to live without your best friend. But you have to grow during hard times or get left behind. So growing we are, and having my husband by my side helps. It just isn't the same when we go shopping, or horseback riding, or riding in the jeep. There is less giggling, less singing at the top of our lungs, and less trying to outrun the boys.

Hannah Cross

I was the second child born to my parents, preceded by my brother of three years. I can tell you that I was born in Ohio, though most of my childhood memories do not begin until I moved to the great state of Minnesota when I was five years old. I remember my first time setting foot on Minnesotan soil quite clearly. My father had hauled us all to our new home in a small town called Orr, Minnesota and it just so happened to be the dead of winter; minus forty degrees fahrenheit if I recall correctly. We had just driven an ungodly amount of hours from our previous apartment in Colorado Springs, Colorado. I was wearing shorts and a t-shirt. When my mother tells this story she likes to emphasize the part where she claims she almost killed my father for taking her and two toddlers to the godforsaken badlands of northern Minnesota in the middle of winter. We survived the freezing temperatures nonetheless and I would spend the majority of my childhood and adolescence in the small village of Orr. My hometown was small, a population of two hundred forty-nine people and decreasing last time I checked. My class was small too, though I was never really bothered by that. I met my best friend in kindergarten. We conquered high school together and even excelled through undergrad. We went on our separate paths afterwards, my future career finding me enrolled in a college of pharmacy in Ohio and her in a college of dentistry in Nebraska. We are still best friends to this day despite the distance between us. I imagine we will still be best friends tomorrow, too.

I have always been a goal-oriented person. In high school the goal was to graduate and go to college to become a pharmacist. In undergrad the goal was to fulfill my pre-pharmacy prerequisites in order to enroll in a college of pharmacy. In pharmacy school the goal was to graduate and enlist in the military and see the world. Remember how I said that my hometown and high school were very small? I realized just how small when I went to undergrad. Now when I say small, I am referring to the class size and the number of peers I had, though the point isn't really quantitative. As a small school, we had limited educational opportunities available to us. I was ranked number one out of thirty two students my senior year of high school. In undergrad the numbers skyrocketed. I wasn't number one anymore. That first semester was the toughest. Everyone else was at the starting line when undergrad classes began while I was ten feet back. I had never seen half the material covered in my first semester of chemistry and I dare not even tell you about physics. I came home for the weekend halfway through my first semester of undergrad to visit my parents. When Sunday rolled around I had packed up the car and was ready to leave when I hugged my parents and started crying. I broke down in front of them. I remember the feeling; all the stress that I was trying to cope with just came rushing out all at once. I told my parents that for the first time in my life I might fail a class in school. I told my parents that I was so afraid of failing. I told them that college was too hard and I just wasn't smart enough. My dad hugged me a moment, then took a step back and he said to me, "Do you remember when Tucker (Tucker being my horse) bucked you off your saddle when you were riding him in the paddock? You hit your bottom and sat there wondering if you were supposed to be scared or pissed off. I'm pretty sure you were a little bit of both, but you jumped right up to your feet and hopped right back into that saddle and you made him listen to you. School is a lot like riding horses. You ride enough horses and one of them will buck you off and every time they do you have to get back in that saddle and show that horse you're not afraid of him". My father is one of the few people I know will always have an answer, even if it's not the one I'm looking for. Yeah, it was a corny analogy, but at the time it was exactly what I needed to hear. With the conclusion of that first semester I ended up passing my chemistry class with an A+ and I would end my undergraduate career with a GPA of 3.8. I faced the same problem with pharmacy school and although I cannot say that I was able to maintain my A+ spree, I have passed all my classes thus far with a B average and I cannot give all the credit to myself.

    I am where I am today not only because of what I have done, but because I have had many family and friends helping me along the way. The hard work it has taken was my doing, but the confidence and encouragement was a gift from those who love me the most. It's funny how, when you stop to think about it, we always have everything we need when we need it. I needed courage to know that I must never fear the challenges before me. My father gave that to me and to this day I have never admitted to being afraid of any of life's curve balls. I think it took a lot of courage for my father to move his family up to the cold, tough terrain of northern Minnesota. My father might be many things, but I would think he would be the first to tell you that he is no fortuneteller. He didn't know if he could make a home and a life in Minnesota. He didn't know that the pharmacy he bought would flourish and provide for him and his family. I didn't know if I could pass my chemistry class in undergrad and get the GPA I needed to enroll in pharmacy school. All we can do is try. Maybe you won't make it the first time, but you'll never make it if you never try, right? In conclusion, may you always look forward to the next challenge and if for some reason you can't find the courage then I hope whatever it is 'pisses you off enough' to make you want to get back in the saddle again.

Ashley Franks

What *does it mean to me to be female?* If you had asked me that a few years ago, I wouldn't have had a response, which is rare for me because I always have a response. The reason I would not have had a response is because I associated female with feminine and that is the thing I least wanted to be associated with. Let's see, my first nickname was pizza face because I ate my favorite food very messily and I could out eat the boys, which is something my dad was always proud of me for. I was the very definition of a tomboy growing up and that is the way I like to be seen. I remember the first time my dad described me as being like his first-born son. I'm probably one of the few girls on this planet that would view that remark as a compliment. "Don't worry about my girl, she can handle herself," he would say. I can't even count the number of times I have heard my dad say that. I focused on being tough, and when I was younger, I didn't feel like I could be considered feminine and tough at the same time. I was rough and tough, and I made sure that was well known.

I have learned so much over the years, and I have realized that there is more than one way to be "tough". There is most definitely more than one way to be female or feminine as well. My problem with answering this question would have been that I saw being female in the stereotypical way. Femininity has nothing to do with wearing dresses. It is not sugar and spice and everything nice.

So now that we have discussed everything that being female does not mean to me, let's discuss what it does mean to me. Being female to me means being exactly who I am. I don't have to fit into a mold to be feminine. It is possible to be a strong, confident, beautiful, and tough woman. As I have grown up, I have learned so much about myself including that the label I most avoided as a child is not so bad. It isn't something to be feared or avoided; it is actually something to be proud of.

I think the other young women that you are growing up with play a huge role in developing the young woman you become. I am very fortunate to have come from a large family. I had two sisters and many female cousins growing up that I was extremely close to. We of course all had family similarities, but we also varied greatly in many ways. We were quite a bunch, tomboys all the way down the line to absolute "girly" girls and just about every combination in between. We learned that having such a variety could work out for the best; we learned to fill in the gaps for each other. A few are artistic, a few are fashionable, a few are outspoken, a few are spontaneous, and a few are athletic and so on and so forth. I have bits and pieces of these wonderful women in the woman that I have become. My oldest sister taught me to be outspoken and protective. My middle sister taught me how to find and express my own creativity even though I'm definitely not artistic like she is. I have a few cousins who encouraged an adventurous side in my personality, even though my idea of adventure is still much more timid than theirs. I have yet another cousin responsible for showing me the courage it takes to go down a daunting, yet rewarding educational path. And a few others responsible for encouraging my "girly" side on the rare occasion that I actually let it out.

I have also learned so much about how to be a strong woman from my mom, an obvious place you would think. We have been through some extremely rough times together, but at the end of the day, she always knows who she is. Everything else in our lives can be uncertain and out of control, but she will just exude confidence and stability. Growing up, I always felt that she knew what to do to handle any given situation. I asked her once how she is always so certain of what needs to be done to keep moving forward past the most unthinkable obstacles. How does she always know what to do to get us through those tough times? She let me in on the secret; she doesn't actually know how to fix all the problems that thrust themselves in our path or even the best course of action in every situation. She simply decides how to fix the problems that have to be fixed at that particular moment and if she continues to do that, then step by step, the long term solution seems to come from all of the short term ones that she has already made. I thought that was remarkably wise. I have since tried to maneuver past life's hurdles with this philosophy and with a little faith, as well as her wisdom, obstacles don't always seem quite as unmovable as they once did. She is the perfect example of a strong, confident woman. I have learned so much from her about how to be my own woman as well.

My brother would be the less obvious place to gain insight on being a strong female. As odd as it sounds, taking care of my brother has taught me so much about myself. If you want to know who you really are, try to help someone else learn who they should grow to become. In trying to teach him how to be himself, I have learned so much by taking my own advice that I gave to him. It is ironic how much more confidence you develop and how much easier it seems to happen when you are aware that it is not just your life and future on the line, but someone else's as well. My little brother needs strength from me in ways I am not always sure I can provide, but it is somehow easier to summon the necessary courage and strength when you know that someone who loves and depends on you absolutely needs you to. My brother is the best thing that has ever happened in my life for this and so many other reasons.

I think the most important part of becoming female for me was simply learning that it is okay to just be yourself. You don't have to fall into a stereotype to be female; you have to make becoming a woman your own. You simply have to decide who you are and what it means to be female for you.

Kelly Dillon

I have learned that many of the life challenges I have experienced happen to many other women. The main things that hit home for me were the fact that many other women also experience GI issues, and that many women struggle in their relationships with their mothers. It's comforting to know that others go through the same challenges. My stomach problems started out off and on for a couple months, and my family doctor wanted to start me on random medications to alleviate pain and cramping I was having.

When symptoms didn't resolve, I had to push to get a referral to a gastroenterologist, and it is frustrating that the medical field can be so hard to deal with, and it helps me better understand why some patients at the pharmacy get so frustrated with the whole process. It took various tests and about a year of doctor's visits to determine I had lymphocytic colitis, a form of colitis usually only found in adults over fifty years old and I was very grateful that I had an aggressive doctor that chose to do the biopsy even though on the surface everything appeared normal. Doctor's visits still continue for me because this form of colitis is usually only seen in older adults, and if it is found in younger adults it is usually due to the presence of Celiac's disease. My blood work has tested negative for Celiac's, but I continue to have symptoms. Going through this whole process definitely helps me relate to patients better because it is tiring and frustrating to not have answers, and to feel like you might be crazy because there are no answers to your problem.

I also learned I could relate to other women when it comes to my relationship with my mother. Looking back at my relationship with my mom I feel has helped me grow as an individual. My mom was always a strong individual, because she was essentially a single mom most of my life, and it taught me to not rely on men and to get things done on my own. Because of this we also butted heads a lot, and because of that I've lived on my own since I was nineteen and things between us are better that way. Due to this I feel I know how to take care of myself and am very responsible because I've been on my own for a long time.

 These experiences have helped shape who I am today, and though they can be rough to experience, they only make you stronger in the long run.

Danielle Heideman

I was raised in a devout Catholic family just as my mom was raised in a devout Catholic family. I am the oldest of my siblings and cousins just as my mom was the oldest and my grandmother was the oldest. I am proud to be a strong stubborn woman like both of them.

My mom was my biggest influence on me when it came to figuring out what it meant to be a woman. As young teens in the youth group at Church we were taught that being a good Catholic woman meant being like Mary, the mother of Jesus. She was a virgin, a good mother, and a good wife. My mom succeeded at all three of those things and is a very good role model on living virtuously. I failed at being a virgin when I was sixteen. At that age, the world revolves around that boy who has convinced you that he loves you. My dad always teases me about how much I missed out on high school because all I wanted to do was focus on that boy. He doesn't know that I had convinced myself that losing my virginity wouldn't matter as long as I married the boy I lost it to. So I unsuccessfully spent four years trying to make him love me. He was a terrible boyfriend. He was happiest when he could convince me that I had wronged him in some way so that I owed him something. He was disrespectful, inconsiderate, and had bad breath. It took four years for me to finally forgive myself, figure out that I didn't need to subject myself to that, and walk away. I deeply regret the choice to have sex at sixteen and thank God it didn't result in a pregnancy that would surely have ruined my life. I have spent the past eight years making my parents believe that I am still a virgin, simply because I can't imagine my mom's disappointment. My sister and I are just now starting to get close enough that we might be able to share things like that with each other. Last year, my best friend Sarah married her high school sweetheart after five years of abstinence together (and serving as her Maid of Honor was one of the proudest moments of my life). I plan to be honest with my children about my life and let Aunt Sarah talk to them about "waiting" so that I won't be a hypocrite.

My parents were married for five years before they had me. For the first year of my life, my mom and I lived on a Navy base in Virginia while my dad was out at sea. Based on the pictures and limited memories, I know that when he came home we were best friends. I looked forward to him coming home and reading to me every night. I really believe all the reading my parents and grandparents did to me when I was little is the reason I ended up being good in school. In third grade, Mrs. Roope saw me reading American Girl books at my desk and thought I was skipping out on the assignment. I was actually done early with my work and reading to pass the time while everyone else finished. Needless to say, I plan to read to my kids every day. Around twelve years old, Dad went from being my best friend to someone I wanted nothing to do with. The only explanation was hormones. I know it hurt his feelings when I would walk in the door and up to my room without greeting him, but he was a trooper. Not wanting anything to do with my dad ended with puberty and more recently we have gotten back to having a good relationship. It can't be easy being the only guy in a house of opinionated women.

When I was five years old, my sister had just been born so my mom had put her engagement ring in her jewelry box so it wouldn't scratch her when she was changing her diapers. I wanted to play wedding with the little girl from next door and we obviously needed a ring if it was going to be realistic. I was a very responsible little groom so I put the ring in the breast pocket of my little yellow polo shirt. The next thing I remember is my parents calling me in to their room a few days later asking where her ring was. I remember my dad helping me look through my room for the little yellow shirt and when we couldn't find it asking my mom where it was. Days before, she had gone through my room and thrown out some of my outdated clothes including the little yellow shirt with her engagement ring in the pocket. Growing up, I knew that what happened that day hurt her. But now, as I am thinking of engagement rings more and more, I can't believe I took such an important symbol from her. I'm at a really special point in my life where I have found the person I want to marry.

He is the most caring person I've ever met. He loves me the way I feel I deserve to be loved and he appreciates me in a way no one ever has. I have always been good at being a girlfriend and I've dated a couple guys who didn't appreciate me until I was gone. Andrew made it obvious that I was his number one priority from day one. Looking forward to seeing him on the weekends is what gets me through the long weeks. And looking forward to spending my life with him is what gets me through the long years. I think the greatest complement a woman can get is to have a man ask her to marry him—for this guy to go from dating you because he is interested in the possibility of a future with you to putting a ring on your finger because he can no longer imagine anything that would make him happier. As long as these 8 years seem, the days really do pass quickly and there is still so much to look forward to on the other side.

Thinking about what it means to be female requires consideration of what makes us different from men. We are better at expressing ourselves and opening up and listening to others. I think that makes us powerful. I went to a lecture recently where the presenter said that they would sometimes recommend one chemo drug over another because the doctor would be more comfortable with it and that you sometimes have to "treat the doctor with the patient". I thought that was interesting and it reminded me of how women sometimes have to encourage a man in a certain way that makes him feel as though he is the one making a decision. Maybe this skill makes us better adept at being pharmacists. I've recently been weighing my options with residency versus job search and I think it is unfair that I have a biological clock ticking away at me as I consider another year of training. Men don't have that problem. Unlike the guys in the class, I have to decide if I want to postpone marriage and starting a family another year. I think it is a woman thing and not just a "me" thing to always be thinking about the future. I feel that for the past seven years, everything I've done has been focused on the future.

Two summers ago my friends and I took a cross-country road trip to Wyoming. It was one of the best times of my life. Looking back, I think the reason it was so enjoyable is that there was no thought of the future. We were living for the moment, taking in everything we possibly could and making the most of every stop. I look forward to graduation and the end of my training to finally be able to stop planning and just enjoy the life I've been given.

Anonymous Author

Growing up, I was always the girl that had it all together. I knew what I was doing after school, where I would go to college and what I would be when I grew up. Nothing out of the ordinary ever truly happened while I was growing up in a small town with a great family. There were, of course, those "rebellious" moments I had that were very short lived. I put rebellious in quotations because my definition of rebellious was getting my belly button pierced when I was eighteen (old enough to sign for myself, it didn't even require a lie). My parents never had to worry about me. They trusted me. I had earned it.

Looking back on those "best years of your life" during high school, I was doing all the right things, taking all of the advanced classes, and dating the star athlete of not only football, but basketball and track, too. We had been together for a total of about five years before we finally graduated high school and went our separate ways. We experienced getting our driving licenses together, went to prom together, and even went to undergrad together. He was one of my closest friends and I look back wishing I could have thanked him for that. Trust me, we definitely had our moments when he was making bad decisions and I had finally realized that we just weren't meant to be. We were *so* young.

Fast forward a few years and I was married and my high school sweetheart was also married. I wouldn't say we were necessarily friends, but definitely acquaintances with a tremendous history ... certainly unforgettable. His family went to my church and his mom always loved me and she thought that one day we would end up back together. I think there was even some resentment when

I reluctantly sent their family a wedding invitation. No RSVP's were received and I just assumed that they had decided as a family that it wasn't the best choice considering out pasts. Nevertheless, his mother showed up at my wedding. My mother still tells me she figured his mom came hoping at the very last second that I would change my mind and go running back to her son. I guess I should just give him a fake name ... we'll call him Joe. So, I was married. Joe was married. Life was good.

On another note, I feel somewhat guilty for even writing about Joe. I'm not really sure why. I am married and have an amazing husband and could wish for nothing more! I would never divulge my thoughts and feelings to intentionally hurt my husband. Ahhh ... I feel better now just by saying that. I just wanted to be clear. This is something that I have never shared before so I'm hoping it will be therapeutic or something.

Okay, so back to being married and Joe being married. During my third year of pharmacy school my husband and I had gone to southeastern Ohio to visit family for the weekend. Like many weekends, I went to my parent's and he went to his. Saturday evening he called to tell me that Joe was in a bad car accident. He knew no details which I figured was a good thing. I muttered a quick prayer under my breath and continued on with my evening plans to take my niece out for a movie. As I drove to pick her up, I kept thinking about Joe and hoping he was okay. He had to be. I walked up the steps and rang the doorbell. My niece answered the door and told her two younger sisters to go to their rooms for a while because she needed to tell me something. I quickly interrupted her and said, "I know, I know. Joe was in an accident. I know he's in the hospital. I know what's going on, we can go now." She responded saying, "He didn't make it." This did not make sense. It couldn't be true. I gasped and said, "What?!" She again repeated those dreaded, forbidden words. I don't do death. I don't handle it, especially when it's in reference to someone that was a huge part of my life. Someone had kicked me in the stomach. I could not breathe. I collapsed on the couch sobbing uncontrollably. This could not be true. I kept picturing him lying on some cold, sterile hospital bed all alone. His eyes wouldn't open. Why couldn't I hear his voice one more time? Why couldn't I make out his face or remember the sound of his voice? Why? Why? Why?

Needless to say, the next few days were beyond horrible. The day following his death, I forced myself out of bed and went to church. His entire family walked in together holding hands. My uncontrollable sobbing started all over again. This could not be real. I tried to be strong especially for his mom. She just kept hugging me and telling me she couldn't imagine life without him. I couldn't either. That sounds completely ridiculous even as I am writing it. What was I thinking? I was being so selfish! How could I be this upset? He wasn't my husband! But I was hurting ... the hurt was so intense. This is when the guilt began to sink in.

The day of the calling hours was upon me and I made the trip to the church. The line extended beyond the double doors and into the parking lot. I wanted to be there to show my support but at the same time, I wanted nothing more than to turn around and run away. I didn't want to see his mom and dad. I didn't want to see his widow. I just did not want this to be my reality. I didn't want to be broken again and again by their tears and hollowed eyes. I just didn't.

Two hours later, I hesitantly walked towards Joe's mom. She hugged me and we both cried. She kept saying he was such a good boy. I knew that already. After more hugs and tears, I was face-to-face with his wife. As I hugged her and cried some more I was directly facing Joe, laying there with that all too familiar smirk. I longed to reach out and touch his arm, squeeze his hand. But I couldn't. He wasn't my husband. I had to be strong. It felt like an eternity that Joe's wife and I were embracing in a way that I never thought possible, considering my history with Joe. I felt like I was hurting just as much as she was but this couldn't be possible, right? But I just couldn't fathom how anyone could be feeling any more pain than I was. Just another thought that even now seems ludicrous. I have no idea if this is even comprehensible to anyone who may read this. These feelings of pain and guilt were almost overwhelming. It was a vicious cycle of pain due to tears, then self-loathing due to those feelings.

All this time I was so consumed with my own sadness, devastation and guilt. It wasn't until my dad approached me that my eyes were opened to something I had not yet considered. He told me that it was okay to be sad and hurting, but that I should be careful not to hurt my husband in the process. He said that he didn't want me to lose sight of what I currently have. I was reminded at that moment that my husband is the most amazing, giving and selfless person I know. He is my better half. I could not imagine life without him. I had not even taken a second to think about or ask him how this entire tragedy was affecting him. I was only drowning in my own sorrow. I soon discussed this with him and being the understanding man that he is, he was okay with my grieving. He said it was normal. My past with Joe was and always will be a part of my life. He let me know that this was okay. He was more than supportive and made me realize how thankful I was for such a great relationship.

It has been just over six months since Joe died and I can honestly say that not a day has gone by that I haven't thought about him. I've always been afraid to say that out loud. It brings back those feelings of guilt again. But it's the truth. The feelings and thoughts I have aren't those of love and lust, but what hurts the most is just that he's not here. If I ever wanted to call him (which I probably wouldn't) I can't. He wouldn't answer. There are so many things I wish I would have had the chance to tell him. He has appeared in my dreams a few different times since his death. It's such an odd thing. I had never dreamed of him ever before. It wasn't until after he was gone that I had such vivid dreams. You know the kind of dream that you just never want to end. In my dreams I just wanted to make sure he was okay. I don't know if anyone will ever understand my thoughts or feelings and maybe no one is meant to. This is still something I deal with on a daily basis and have a feeling that I will continue to struggle.

Through all of this, I have learned that even though my life was pretty routine growing up, it still managed to be turned upside down when I thought everything was flowing along seamlessly. I'm still the girl with the wonderful friends, family, and husband that are the glue that holds my world together. I'm still the girl that has everything together and all my ducks in a row. The ducks feathers are just slightly ruffled now.

Anonymous Author

We are *all here together to help one another on our journey of evolution to be the best person we can be.* Life takes work". Suzanne Somers' shared this sentiment when she was talking about her experiences growing up. I felt her story to be very inspiring and I felt a strong emotional connection to her words. She grew up in worst scenario possible. On the other hand, I feel very grateful because I was loved by my family. Even though I love my dad from the core of my heart, it is hard to forget the moments when he dominated my mother. I think it's a feeling of helplessness that bothers me the most. The times where we want to take over and make everything right. Suzanne Somers' talked about hitting her dad and even if violence was not the best action to take, it made her feel strong and in control. I was reminded of my own struggling times. There were moments when I had to stand up for myself. Some people warned me to step back because they said sometimes we have to adjust to the situation. However, there were those times I felt that taking my power back was the best thing to do. The consequences were in my favor, and even now, whenever I feel weaker, I remind myself of those times and it brings me back the lost confidence. I am reminded to believe in myself, my strengths, and capabilities. Through all of my worst times I am reminded that it is in my hands to shape my own future.

I love to cook and I have a dream of opening up my own restaurant. It would be a restaurant with an international blend of Indian, Mexican, Thai, and I am still exploring more. Whenever I share this idea with my dad, he shuts me up by telling me to focus on what I am doing and not get sidetracked. Sigh! There goes my dream. It's just an example of how difficult is to keep the happiness and dreams alive. It is easy to lose sight of that which makes us happy in the times of stress and the havoc that inhabits our own world.

I am actually elated when I read stories about other women, looking at how strong other women have been in times of challenge and how much they have achieved makes me feel empowered. I don't think that these were just the "chosen ones". I believe all women feel a connection as they relate to other stories of women struggling to find their inner spirit. I feel more connected with fellow women and comforted by the fact that we all have much in common despite skin color, ethnicity or religion.

Life takes work. We all struggle from different insecurities and hardships. We all fight for the better life, even though it may not the best way to do it. Perhaps it is our way and that alone makes it okay. Maybe we just have to believe in ourselves and start from a place within ourselves. It's never going to be easy, and maybe it should never be.

Preet Bajwa

Growing up female for me means thinking about my past every single day. When I was seven years old, I was molested by my babysitter. I still re-live the events of that day in my mind. It has been twenty-three years and I can still remember what I was wearing that day; a light blue and white plaid dress with a white lace collar. The incident only happened once, but it was enough to scar me for the rest of my life. I used to think that it was my fault because my dress was perhaps a little too short, maybe I was too friendly, or maybe it was my fault because I put myself into that situation; falling asleep on the lap of a teenage boy who was supposed to look out for me.

Later that evening, my sister and I told a family friend what happened. This person then told my parents. All I remember is that mom went over to yell at him and my dad saying, "You better not be making this up". I resented my mom for a long time afterwards, why didn't she do more besides yell? I felt like she let me down and that she had failed to protect me from people like that. Even though I remember this happening, I honestly don't really know if my parents know or if they want to know what happened. We never talk about it. It's like some deep family secret that no one brings up.

Just this April, I found out my sister was also abused by the same person. For all these years I was grateful that it had happened to me and not to her because I was the strong one. I thought that she would never be able to handle this and besides I was supposed to take care of her and protect her since I was the older twin. My sister and I have since talked about our past. What I realize is that sometimes really bad things happen to good people.

Every time I think about what happened, I'm giving this predator a piece of me and I can't give him that satisfaction. Talking about this has enabled me to move on, let go, and not carry this baggage with me any longer.

Anonymous Author

I never really understood what it meant to grow up but I think I have a pretty good idea now thanks to Maya Angelou. She said it so perfectly that it captures the whole essence of what it is to be a grown-up. She said that to grow up is to be in a perpetual state of forgiving; forgiving yourself and forgiving others. To grow up is to be selfless. To grow up is to cherish every opportunity of friendship and know in your heart that you may never see these people ever again. To grow up is to know that you will eventually leave behind everyone you loved and cared for and everything you worked very hard for and ask yourself, "How can I be of use to people around me while I'm still here?"

I've been accused many times for taking life way too seriously. I can't escape the urge to find meaning in virtually anything that affects me emotionally. Some friends have said that I worry or think too deeply about things that aren't going to change anything. But that's not true. I can be shallow too and worry about my age like all women do. Last summer I turned thirty and I thought it was going to be the worst. I felt old already and I didn't feel like I had accomplished anything in my life. I had been thinking about turning thirty even years before but when it finally happened, the sun was still shining and life went on. Is this a female thing? To worry about things constantly; to have the need to care for other people? And at the same time being afraid of getting old and looking old. Having said that, I'm not so sure anymore if I am really growing up or I'm just feeling the need to grow up. Most of the friends I grew up with have kids and for them the need to care and love unconditionally is being fulfilled by having a family. Maybe I'm thinking this way because I don't have a responsibility to raise children. Maybe I'm feeling guilty for thinking about no one but myself and my needs for as long as I can remember.

In retrospect, I had no choice but to take care of "numero uno" because neither of my parents bothered to raise me. I grew up with my maternal grandparents and my parents never attended any of my graduation from elementary to high school, not a single Christmas, or any of my birthdays. I didn't really know my mom until we got together later in my teens. From my perspective, she failed as a mother. I never really understood why things happened the way they did and I never questioned them. I was convinced that I was nothing but an inconvenience to her and that my needs were not as important as hers. Even though my mother and I have a better relationship now, I'm not so sure I have fully forgiven her. My relationship with her ebbs and flows as it has for many years.

Life feels so great during the times when my mother and I are on good terms. I feel at ease even when things aren't going so well because I feel her motherly presence. But the feelings of such comfort are always overshadowed by feelings of awkwardness. This is probably because I'm not used to her motherly role in my life and even though I revel in these feelings, the unfamiliarity prevents me from moving forward.

I try not to think about having been molested. It was part of the biggest reason why I despised my mother when I was growing up. I believe it was her duty to protect me but she was never around. Because of her absence, no one was there to console me when I needed it. But I need to grow up, and to grow up is to be in a perpetual state of forgiving, forgiving myself and others. And I have come to terms with the realization that this includes my mother.

Anonymous Author

When *I think of becoming myself, I think of a deeply troubled soul who is still on a path of searching for the true answer of happiness.* Finding out why I am the way I am required some deep soul searching. Something that can be hard to talk about and has always been a piece of my life's puzzle of insecurities and distrust comes from me being put in a foster home as a child. This is where I found out the cruelties of life.

Although I did not have the best home with my mother, I was happy there. We did not always have the best food to eat but we made what we could of it. I remember a time when we only had a bag of potatoes so we made fries, baked potatoes, mashed potatoes, whatever you can think of. I don't want my mom to look bad in any way because I love her to death but there was a dark period in our lives when she became a really bad mom. She put her selfishness in front of her children causing us to go through things kids should not have to endure. I have seen things as a child most people will never see in their lifetime. I have witnessed a man being stabbed and domestic violence on a routine basis. My mom was irresponsible and even after receiving a second chance we were put into one of my worst nightmares, a foster home.

Foster homes are places where kids are supposed to go to be protected not go through more abuse and neglect. One thing I can say is that we were fed (although the food sucked) but our clothes and hygiene were absolutely awful. I just wanted some nice pretty clothes and shoes like the rest of the kids. So one day I asked my foster mom if I could have better clothes because the ones she dressed us in were ugly. It is not that I needed the nicest clothes but the clothes were outdated and just plain ridiculous. Her response to me was "Well, you are ugly." I have never forgotten that and for a long time I thought I was this ugly creature. In my opinion this is surely mental abuse. I became insecure and would ask everyone if they thought I was ugly for years. I would cry over how ugly I was and everyone would get mad at me for it.

When I told my mom and dad of this they said I am far from ugly. When I would tell others what this mean old lady said, they said she must have been jealous but honestly I believe she thought I was ugly either in looks or personality. When a child has already been through so much why would you make them feel any worse? My mom did not understand how this affected me and said I am just too sensitive and I should grow some "thick skin."

Although I am still growing to become myself, the self I am right now is still affected by her calling me ugly. I do not trust people easily. I know as time goes on hopefully this will no longer affect me. I want my children to know how important and beautiful they are everyday! If anyone calls them anything than what they are, they will know better because their parents instilled in them otherwise. They will have good clean clothes and great hygiene.

Chennel Hill

Growing up female is an intense and sometimes mind blowing adventure that never seems to end. Females are constantly reinventing themselves to adapt and accomplish any new twist and turn in life, but in order to do that you have to have a firm grasp on who you are as an individual. That is where my story comes in. All young children when growing up go through phases when they try to figure out who they are. You look to your parents, friends, and siblings to try to identify with and find some insight into who it is you are supposed to fit in with. As a young child I struggled with just that. I knew at a very young age I was different from my other African American classmates and the attributes that made me different made some people hate me even more. Growing up in the south where race still seemed to matter at that time, I noticed that one race was definitely considered superior to the other. I could see that my fair skinned mom had more advantages then my darker skinned father. Even though I loved them both equally, I knew that to look more like my mother was a better option even though I couldn't quite accomplish that. I struggled through everything from hair styles (braids when I played with my black friends and straight hair with my white friends), to the clothes I would wear. One day I figured the African American classmates were more welcoming because there insults were fewer and less hurtful than others. Besides in the south, one ounce of African American in your blood made you black, even if you were mixed with other races. I had to explain why my hair was long, and why my eyes were green/hazel. To my white or black friends I just didn't look black enough. I really wish I could find the person that defined what it meant to "look" black. I cringed at grandparents' day at school, because each time my grandparents came to marvel at their grandkids accomplishments it was like my secret was revealed. I spent that time at recess explaining to my friends why my grandfather was white, and my grandmother was black, what that made my mom, and what that made me. It was just easier to dismiss the white side of my family and just say. "Hey I'm black like you." I felt I had to be two different people to fit in with each race and I ended up just being confused.

When my family and I moved to Ohio and I started high school, it seemed to escalate. It was always "You should wear your hair straight because it makes you look more white", or my black friends would say, "Why don't you wear your hair curly because it makes you look more black? "Where is your attitude? Black people have an attitude. You can't be black if you don't act, talk or walk this way". Again what does that even mean? I thought it was supposed to be better here, since it seemed like in the northern states having to identify with one race was not as important. One day my little sisters came home and said that everyone at school said that our mom couldn't be our mother because she was white. That night we had "that conversation". My mom began to explain everything about racism and I thought I already know this. Why is she talking about this again? But then she said something that finally clicked with me. She said why should I have to identify with one race when God saw fit to bless me with more than one? She said very simply, I am who I am and anyone that doesn't see past the color of your skin to acknowledge you as a human being is not worth your time. God didn't make us to fit in with anyone, he made us to be unique in our own way and that's how you should be.

From then on I never worried again what I was or struggled to identify with one group of people, because in the end it doesn't really matter. I stopped trying to "act like a race" and just let naturally who I was begin to take root and develop into its own style. I began to talk with my grandmothers and found that there were a lot of other races mixed in our family as well. I figured who has time to mark all those boxes on a survey anyway? I'm so proud to have the wonderful mix that is "me" and I laugh when people sit and stare to figure out what races make up my mix. Yes, it is many different pieces, but they all come together to make one wonderful picture!

My advice to other ladies growing up female in a world that tries put you in a box, stay out of the box! You are who you are, so walk proud and be confident in who that person is, the rest of the world will just have to deal with it.

Anonymous Author

Bitch—*there I have said it.* Yes, I understand, fairly forthcoming. Frank even. I get it—we females are supposed to be *dainty*. Demureness and this image of a lady are contradicted when a female has a "sailor's mouth". Well, shit, guess we don't have those standards and expectations between us now do we?

That being said, let us delve into the grit. The term bitch and I have a love-hate relationship. Such a measly little word—simple even, with five letters—should never hold such power. Yet, it does. It transcends a word put on paper. It defines the tone of a conversation; can begin an argument. So much power, in one word. However, the beauty of this word is that it is specifically used for females. Think of this—one word alone described for the female gender. I love it. It's like a secret only females share. Let me explain ...

I remember the first time I was called a bitch. I was in second grade. A school mate was displeased with something my ignorant eight-year-old self did. And what did I do? Go crying to the teacher, and the boy was reprimanded. I remember my eight-year-old self was satisfied with this punishment and went along with my daily papers. However, I will never forget how upset I was in that one moment. What would have precipitated such a mean name-calling?

Little did I know, this term would be constantly reintroduced into my personal dictionary. This second-grade, quiet version of me was just a phase. Puberty hit and suddenly I found sarcasm, wit, a voice that never stopped talking, and a strong passion for success. I knew I wanted to be a leader, in the forefront; I just needed the experience to get me there. Throughout my teens, I was outspoken, opinionated, and saw a future that I strove for on a daily basis. Again, bitch became a frequent term aimed my way.

I took leadership positions; I beat out my male-counterparts. I rocked the boat with my tendencies towards the logical over the emotional. I am not saying this is the only way to be successful as a female, I am merely saying this was my way. It was slightly off-putting for some. Others laughed. Still, I was an oddity. I was honest, and I would be to the point of others getting insulted. My friends joked I had more testosterone floating in my system than estrogen. To my face, people would call me ignited, behind my back, I was a bitch.

So I divert, why are these characteristics—outgoing, forthright, driven, and goal-oriented—considered male characteristics? Why must the desire for success be classified as masculine? What am I supposed to do, sit home and watch the children and speak only when addressed? I have way too many opinions for that.

I laugh when I think of how different individuals have conversed with my boyfriend, of almost three years, and me. Often, they turn to me, asking, "Oh! No ring? When are you guys getting married anyway?" Almost in the next instant, they will turn to him asking about how his medical education is fairing. How is this double standard acceptable? The irony is I will have a doctorate before he has his.

Or take for instance, when my career plans are discussed. Pharmacy? That is such a great career for a woman to work part time! Why would I waste the sweat, the hard work, and the time to merely raise a family? Again, this is no slight to those who chose to do this—I recognize how difficult it is—but again, I restate, why would one even begin to think that is my motive for entering the field? No one would ever say that to my boyfriend. The males in my pharmacy class have never heard this. They would laugh. What a silly thought, having a doctorate and a man staying home instead? And thus, it comes full circle. The bitch that has no interest in an early marriage and popping out kids at age 33.

The sad portion of this thought is *we women accept these standards and call each other these names!* It is not men driving these low standards. Women, stand up, we are a force. We allow these standards or else they would not be a barrier. Help each other rise to power. Help each other succeed. Put strong focus on goals. And for God's sake, let your twenties be for yourself!

Let me repeat this last line again, let your twenties be for yourself. Be selfish. Be self-centered. Be who you need to be. Let yourself grow and learn. Women often grow up with the expectation to be a nurturer; for everyone else. Nurture yourself in your twenties. You will be labeled a bitch. People will take it as a female willing to step over anyone to get to a specific position. Who cares? Do things for you. Develop into a strong young female who is independent and loves the person she is. Do not get swallowed up in the guilt.

This time is difficult. It can be emotional and tiring. Thus, my advice is to surround yourself with other strong females, as mentors and peers. These positive, successful women will mold and alter your path. With this network, you are destined for success. I have had the pleasure of surrounding myself with individuals who are insightful, knowledgeable, and always pushing the standards. They inspire me daily. Find these women and embrace them.

And so, this bitch becomes merely a female becoming herself. She is strong. She is conscious of her vision of herself. She is independent. It's beautiful. For those of you who have not been called a bitch, prepare for it. Prepare for the hurt at the beginning but learn and grow from it. For those of you who have had the privilege of being called bitch, embrace it. You are probably doing something right.

A bitch, you say? Why thank you.

Megan Elavsky

As you make the transition into our second set of stories, we would like to share a poem with you. It is about an oyster that takes a grain of sand, life's irritant, and turns it into a beautiful pearl. The wise oyster knows it must embrace this irritant and steadfastly cover the grain of sand with layer upon layer of substance. Only after many years and with much effort has the oyster completely changed its internal environment (perhaps its internal voice) into something beautiful and lasting.

The Oyster And The Pearl

There once was an oyster, whose story I tell,
Who found that some sand had got into his shell.
It was only a grain, but it gave him great pain.
For oysters have feelings, although they're so plain.

Now, did he berate the harsh workings of fate
That had brought him to such a deplorable state?
Did he curse at the government, cry for election,
And claim that the sea should have given him protection?

'No,' he said to himself as he lay on a shell,
Since I cannot remove it, I shall try to improve it.
Now the years have rolled around, as the years always do,
And he came to his ultimate destiny stew.

And the small grain of sand that had bothered him so
Was a beautiful pearl all richly aglow.
Now the tale has a moral, for isn't it grand

What an oyster can do with a morsel of sand?
What couldn't we do If we'd only begin
With some of the things that get under our skin.

Author Unknown

It is actually through hearing the inspiring stories of these women that the title and theme for our book emerged. We hope that you will read and enjoy these stories and perhaps identify with some of them. It may be that they will bring a bit of understanding to your own situations as you realize that you are not alone in the life you are living.

Section 2

The Hallmarks of a Woman

My character has been influenced by many people throughout my life, most notably by several women. They possess several characteristics which I believe are innate to being a woman; qualities we are born with which occur naturally and have a positive impact on those around us. Throughout one's life as a woman, I believe we refine and develop these skills as part of our inner obligation to ourselves, as well as our dedication to leaving a positive impact on others.

Nurturing—If there is at least one thing I can do each day to help make someone else's journey through this life just a bit easier to travel, then I feel the day has been a success. Two women who have consistently demonstrated nurturing qualities throughout my life are my mother and my grandmother. Their generosity, loving nature, and dedication to their family are exemplified in everything that they do. They give selflessly, and expect little to nothing in return. Several other women in my life, mostly friends and professional mentors, have encouraged me to follow my dreams as well, and support me consistently. This fostering environment allows me to thrive and remain positive in all that I do.

Relatability—As women, we have an uncanny ability to relate to others. Whether we are identifying a common interest, feeling the emotion of others by drawing upon past experiences, or seeking advice about a current situation, we are constantly changing our perspective in order to develop and foster new relationships. I frequently communicate with my friends with no predetermined focus of discussion, other than to hear about what has been going on in their lives since we last talked. It is so important to me to know how to continue to develop my relationship as a friend, learn from friends who have experiences to share, and support friends through trials or tribulations that may come about. We attempt to make connections with others, whether by sharing a family tradition, discussing the store in which we just found *the best* sale, or telling a story of struggling through our latest career decision in order to build and establish lasting relationships.

Self-sufficiency—Although interdependence through relationships is an essential part of daily living, several women in my life possess the quality of independence. We can rely on others as part of our day-to-day activities, but women around me whom I admire possess an intrinsic motivation; a purposeful drive that is inspirational and incredible. As a woman, surrounding yourself with other women who are highly independent is moving. This momentum gained by surrounding oneself with ambitious women undoubtedly translates into leading a successful life. Independent women are able to be a productive part of society while balancing an established family and social life outside of the workplace. This well-roundedness allows a woman to be autonomous because she can successfully operate in all worlds simultaneously.

Honestly, most days I don't consider myself to be of any lesser or greater substance than the opposite gender. We all have our differences in personalities, motives, and beliefs. However, that which makes us human is, in my opinion, the same as the male gender. Although we may have intrinsic differences in being a female, we make invaluable contributions to our world which should be recognized equally to contributions made by our male counterparts.

Jackie Kruse

What's Wrong with Women's Rights?

Beatrice Arthur was ranting each week to her husband Walter about equal rights on television as *Maude*. The cast of *Charlie's Angels* brought "jiggle tv" into our living rooms for all to see. Cher was everything a young girl wanted to be, with her tanned and toned body, "Rapunzelesque" hair, and talent. On the *Sonny & Cher* show, her bit was usually to put down Sonny, no matter what he said or did. Poor guy just couldn't win with her. She had a zinger for every occasion.

Television in the 1970s was merely reflecting what was going on in society. On the heels of the civil rights movement, the women's movement was everywhere. Women were asserting themselves as equals to men and rejecting the long-held expectation of becoming only housewives and mothers. In this social climate, I regularly heard statements like these from my mother and grandmother:

"*Go as far as you can go.*"

"*Don't ever rely on a man for anything. Be able to take care of yourself.*"

As an early member of Generation X (aka the MTV Generation), I was born on the tail end of bra burning and women's lib. Hearing these words and seeing these images, one would expect the women of my generation to be bona-fide men haters, but to understand their position, we have to go back in time.

My grandmother was born in 1921. She lived through events that most of us only read about in history class, including the Great Depression and World War II. She was one of twelve children. Her father was a farmer, and as was often the case, the children were the farmhands—the manual labor needed to keep the family from starving. Not starvation like we joke about these days, but literal starvation. Grandma was six feet tall and weighed only 115 lbs! She says the family ate beans and potatoes for lunch, then potatoes and beans for dinner. In addition to being poor, her father would frequently go into town for days at a time to get drunk and leave the family wondering if and when he would come back. There wasn't a lot of security there. Unfortunately for her, most of the older siblings were girls, and only so many were needed to take care of the younger children at the house. Because of this, Grandma labored in the fields, right alongside the men. As a result, she was only allowed to attend school for two years. She went to first grade, and because she was apparently pretty smart, she skipped to fourth grade. Her father felt that this was all the schooling she needed. After all, she was just going to be a housewife. This was a very bitter pill for her to swallow. She very much wanted to attend school, but no matter how much she begged, her father forbade it.

As her life played out, she would be one of the many women who would join the work force while the men were fighting World War II. She worked in the factory for forty-two years before retiring. As a young working wife and mother, she had to leave her children during the workweek with their grandparents in the country while she and my grandfather worked in Cincinnati.

Undoubtedly, Grandma saw this as an opportunity to put food on the table and to be able to enjoy the simple things in life so many of us take for granted, like rugs and curtains. When her children were old enough, all of the family would finally be together in the same house.

Fast-forward to my mother's formative years. She was one of many young teens who raced home to watch *American Bandstand* every day. Elvis Presley was her Justin Bieber. When Mom finished high school, my grandmother made her find something to do with her life other than sit around the house waiting for her Prince Charming to appear. She went to nursing school and got a job while still living at home. She came of age in the time of free love and hippies. Unfortunately, she fell head-over-heels in love with a carpenter who already had a wife (common-law) and children in another county. That didn't stop her. In a very short time she had three children, one right after the other, and a man she was crazy about, but one who had no intention of giving up his other family. He was plenty happy with the way things were; he had his family back home and his family in the city.

Mom left home during her second pregnancy (me). Our dad stayed with her while he had work in town. She realized, one day, that although she was perfectly happy with the time she spent with our dad and could have easily continued living the way they did, she just knew he had no real interest in helping her raise us. She gave him the boot, and as a result, we grew up fatherless. So, my mother continued to work while others raised us, just as her mother had done.

Without even realizing it, listening to these stories

and growing up in this manner truly did have an effect on me. Obviously, there was no real push from my family to get married or have children. Men just weren't reliable, according to them. If we, as women, didn't take care of ourselves, who was going to? I was strongly encouraged to do well in school and to get a job. There was never any talk of "someday when you get married". I certainly didn't set out to get married any time soon. But God has a plan for all of us, and much to my surprise, I went from being a college graduate one week to a new bride the very next. My husband likes to tease that I went to college to get my "Mrs. Degree", but he and I both know that was far from the truth.

In spite of all the talk of women getting established in the work world and putting off having children, my husband and I always knew we wanted children, as many as four! We were twenty-six years old when we thought we would be parents. Again, God has his own plan, and it would be another seven years before our dearest wish would become reality. I was incredibly blessed in the fact that I didn't have to continue working after my daughter was born. There had always been the expectation beforehand that I would work; everyone did, after all. Women were important to the work force! You don't spend all that money to get an education and then just stay home! Funny thing was, I *did* want to stay home with my baby. I relished it. But believe me, I had many challenges to face in making the transition. I imagine that for women of an earlier time, being a wife and mother would be the ultimate fulfillment of their purpose in the world. I knew I didn't want to be anywhere else but home after becoming a mother, but my, was it an adjustment!

I definitely felt, from society's perspective, that I was letting down all the women who had come before me and fought for the right to be more than a man's decoration and caretaker. I felt cut-off from my peers and friends who were still working while raising their families. Yet, as out-of-place and cut-off as I felt, somehow I always knew exactly where I really wanted to be; at home with my children. I was strongly opposed to leaving them for someone else to raise while I worked, as was the case for both my mother and my grandmother.

My daughters are now twelve and ten years old, and I *still* struggle with the decision to stay home. Over the years, I have worked part-time in different capacities since the girls were old enough for preschool. I have had great opportunities to "make something" of myself again, but I always have to walk away because of my self-imposed limits of wanting to be there for my children. It's a daily struggle to deal with the need to be a meaningful part in my children's upbringing and society's expectation for me to "have it all". I'm sorry, but I just can't buy into this theory. You cannot have it all, at least not at the *same time*—either work or family will suffer. For as much as I am a part of the generation of career women (and I am—I think all women should have an education and be able to take care of themselves), I would choose family every time. You see, for me, women's rights have always been about choice. I may not be in the corporate world now, but ultimately, it's because I want to be home with my kids. I wish I didn't always feel judged for this decision. Ironically, I'm probably the one who judges myself the harshest. Interestingly enough, however, neither my mother nor my grandmother batted an eyelash when they found out I wouldn't return to work after having my children. Their approval speaks volumes to me about the women's movement.

My dream for my daughters, is for them to live in a world where they can be happy doing whatever they decide to do with their lives, whether it's to have a career, be a housewife and mother, or all of it! I want them to be able to choose their *own* path without fear of societal backlash or guilt. I want them to not be afraid of being judged when making decisions for their families. These, I believe, are the rights our grandmothers and mothers fought for us to have and enjoy.

Anonymous Author

Attitude of Gratitude

I grew up in a small town and have always been one of those people that can say they have friends they have known their entire lives. I am thankful that I grew up with a handful of girls that experienced life's big stepping stones together in fabulously imperfect ways. We all made mistakes, had heartaches, but each one of us can say that we lived life to the fullest (and probably then some). I am grateful that we got to live and learn from each other while we could.

In a group full of women, it is inevitable everyone has a role to play. Truthfully, I was the fat girl. I'm not saying that to elicit a reaction, I'm simply stating a fact. We were all individuals with specific attributes, and being the "big" girl was my role. I don't think anyone else thought of me that way because we had all been together so long, but when it came to going out, flirting, and dating, it was obvious. We would go out to the club and drink, dance, and have a great time. Men would approach my friends, dance, kiss, and whatever else the night brought, and while no one ever made me feel excluded, I was definitely not getting the flirts, the looks, or the phone numbers that seemed so common with my peers. Naturally, I adapted and (in hindsight) tried to be the life of the party. Coincidentally, my version of that included outrageous amounts of alcohol. Whether I was drinking to have a good time or drinking to ignore that I was, in fact, not being noticed, I will never know.

Throughout my late teens, this behavior continued,

and as I got older, I did finally get attention from men, but I was too excited to notice that it wasn't really the right kind of attention. I fell into a trap of being used. I was so anxious to find someone who wanted to be with me that I would do almost anything to make them happy. I learned, the hard way, that this type of behavior attracts people who are destructive and who get their self-confidence from putting other people down. I dated men who told me that no one else would love me because I was crazy and no one else would sleep with me because I was fat. I stuck around because, after awhile, I believed all those lies. As I look back, I endured years of emotional abuse and gave up things that no one should ever ask another person to give up. At the point of my mid-twenties, my friends were starting to get married, and I found myself picking up my alcoholic boyfriend from jail on Christmas Eve. It's easy for me to look at that situation now and realize that it was unhealthy, but at that time, I thought that this was going to be the best I could do.

A few years later, after moving across the country with that same man I picked up on Christmas Eve, my self-confidence began to grow. I realized that I *am* a good person and that I *don't* deserve to be treated like I am nothing. I moved out on my own and took a break from dating, but as my burst of confidence began to wane, I found friends who would use me instead. I have gained some amazing and supportive friends over the years, but these particular friends were users, taking comfort in other's misery, and I fell back into some old behaviors. I found myself bending over backwards only to be taken advantage of while still calling these people my friends.

While I won't readily admit that I am glad I have been treated badly, I will say that I am thankful that I am now a person that appreciates acts of kindness. I am thankful for a thoughtful gesture, no matter how small, and can barely contain my joy when I see that someone appreciates my effort as well. I shudder to think about the outrageous traumas and horrible treatment that has molded me into an appreciative and giving person, and maybe that's why I am grateful to others with that attitude. After living through emotional abuse and thinking at one point I did not deserve better, I know now I do deserve more and I will never go back to that place again. I realized that I dictate the way others treat me and I will not tolerate people in my life who do not respect and value me. For these lessons, I am grateful. For those who stood by me, loved me and still have my back; you are my lifelong friends.

Kelly Faiola

Love After All

During most of my childhood, my mother was a single mother. She married young, just out of high school. She had my sister at age nineteen, and a year later, I was born. Soon after that my parents divorced. I don't remember my parents ever being together. I barely remember my mom marrying again in a small courthouse ceremony. I think I was about four years old. That marriage brought about my two brothers, six years apart. This husband introduced us to domestic violence and the effects of drug use on a family. Soon after my youngest brother was born, they also divorced. I can't recall very many happy family times when she was married. My mother had custody of all four of us. She didn't believe in depending on a man for survival. She worked full time, never a steady shift. We survived, but I'm not sure how. I can't imagine how difficult it was to shuffle four kids to activities plus manage homework, school projects, sports, dance recitals, band concerts and parent teacher conferences. She even helped with girl scouts and coached softball. I was proud of her for how she handled everything. She depended on my sister and I to do a lot around the house. My sister and I babysat our younger brothers, learned to cook and did other chores. I felt like we helped a lot, but it was probably not enough. It was hard for my mom, but we got by.

Looking back, I did not have a strong role model for a father figure. I'm sure my mother loved both my father and my brothers' father in some way. I don't remember any type of loving relationship between my mother and father, though, as I was too young. I've searched my memories for evidence of any type of outward affection between my mom and my brothers' dad, but I come up empty. I don't remember any hugs between them nor sneaking a kiss when they thought we weren't looking, or any quirky names or hand holding. Either it wasn't there or they hid it from us.

I wasn't close with my father. He also remarried when I was young. His wife had two children of her own. He visited a few times a year and even took us to his house for a week during summer vacation. He moved around a lot for work, so visiting was tough. When we did visit, I would get really homesick and occasionally I went home early. Sometimes I feel like I really missed out on having a relationship with my dad as a child, but I am now finally getting to know him. As an adult, when I spend time with my dad, I realize that we are a lot alike. I finally know where I got my sense of humor.

When I was younger and thought about getting married, I just knew it would be forever. I knew that it was a serious commitment that would sometimes take work. My husband and I started dating in high school. I was young when I married, just like my mother. M husband and I say "I love you" every day, we kiss and hug; we hold hands when we walk, even in public. We call each other "honey" and "dear" and "darling". I hope we are teaching our two beautiful sons that it is healthy to openly love and show affection to your spouse and to your children. We genuinely like to spend time together, as a couple and as a family. We do almost everything together. We have been married for sixteen years, but it doesn't feel like it. I hope that we have fifty or sixty more years together, and I look forward to it. I know that our marriage and family have been blessed and I am thankful for that.

As for my mother, she seems happy most of the time. She is married once again, but this time to a man I call my step dad. They have been married for almost twenty years. He has two daughters that I consider my sisters. I love him like he is my father. I hope she is as happy with how her life has unfolded and her relationships as I am with mine. I don't want to say that I have learned from her mistakes, because her mistakes have taught me about love and marriage and what they mean to me. So I guess they weren't mistakes after all, they were experiences set in place to learn from, and I truly believe that I have learned valuable lessons. Without knowing it, my mom taught me how to love. We just show it in different ways.

Anonymous Author

From Bullied to Bold

All humility aside; I am one of the most popular people on my block, in my community, and I'm well known in my profession. I'm an author, an inspirational speaker, an insightful executive coach, a caring daughter, sister and partner, a contented person as well as good friend to many. People say I'm bold and I am! They say that I'm fun, energetic, considerate and compassionate—I've even been called magnetic! Pretty funny, considering there was a time when I was the least popular person I knew, unless you count being popular for being picked on. Today, you'd never know that I was a bullied little girl.

I was just a normal kid with a good family and strong center. I wasn't ugly or mean or stupid; I wasn't poor, abused or unloved by my parents. But for some reason, I was just one of those kids who somehow ended up with a target painted on my heart and starting at about age ten, the coyotes began circling. I don't really know why. I suppose I never will. I also can't really remember the exact turning point where people who had been my friends my whole life seemed to suddenly turn on me. That's when I became prey; facing four years of what felt like brutal bullying.

I had a teacher, who was part of the problem, and there are certain incidents that really stand out in my mind, but I never knew the real catalyst for incurring the wrath of my peers. Finally, at age 45, I've stopped trying to figure it out. Because it doesn't matter anymore. What matters is that I survived it and I went on to thrive!

The experience, as bad as it was, shaped who I am today in a lot of really great ways. I can't ever say that I'm grateful for the bullying; it's wrong, uncalled for and completely and utterly unacceptable, and it happens far too often to too many kids; one in four to be exact. Back then, I was incredibly sensitive and it hurt like hell. Today, I can say that because of it, I am better and stronger and wiser, not to mention happier and healthier. Probably happier than most of my bullies. The best revenge really is living well!

There is a part of me that always thought I was destined for greatness and in my own little way I found it. Of course, back then, I thought I'd be starring on Broadway! Well Broadway didn't happen, but because of my experiences I was bound and determined to get out of the small town I grew up in. As far as I was concerned, the farther away the better. This allowed me to explore whole new worlds and gave me the gypsy itch to travel and explore new places and cultures. I've been on an adventure ever since. Those experiences helped me to see the world through a set of eyes that lifetime "small towners" don't always use; the eyes of acceptance and tolerance.

Thankfully, my bullying ended when I entered high school; though I never knew why. Maybe there were enough upper classmen who knew and liked me, or maybe it's because Facebook didn't exist back then. I'm sure there were those who still said things behind my back, and I'm sure I carried a bit of an internal grudge. Who could blame me? I wouldn't say I became one of the cool kids in high school, although I became well known for my performance in musicals, with the band, playing softball and on the swimming and diving teams. This was a blessing that was not lost on me.

I went to college in a state far away from my home. There I fit in well and was well-liked by most, so I stayed. Many years later I moved to another state even farther from my home. Some folks back home might say I was running away. I don't believe I was running *from* something but *to* something. Bullying aside, I never really fit in in my hometown. I didn't have the same political and philosophical leanings and I was certainly more open-minded than most of my peers. Today, I could fit-in almost anywhere and yet I still wouldn't go back. It's not who I am. My hometown was a good place to be *from*.

All this is not to say that my life hasn't been without its challenges. I have had career ups and downs, personal losses and at one point I was married to a really good alcoholic for several years. I have been a part of the craziness that is co-dependency, understood first-hand the joys and endless personal summers of menopause and I'm beginning to age in a way that I don't always consider to be graceful. The real point here is that I have lived! I did not just survive those days of bullying. I have lived and I have thrived and I have grown and gotten wiser with every achievement, challenge, mistake and mishap. I have grown bold and have made choices that have shocked some and surprised others. I have become the best person that I can be everyday (and believe me each day is different). I have found the love of my life and I am more in love every day. I am both grateful and blessed.

I believe in being considerate of others, maybe because early on others were not so considerate of me.

I don't believe in accidents and I do believe we make our own luck. I also believe that there is a universal spirit that guides us; and he/she/it may have many names but in the end it doesn't matter what the name is, just that we use our powers for good!

Cindy Coe

Hiding

When I was young, I remember hiding in my room. Once, way up in my closet on a high shelf, I wondered how long I could stay there without being found. I also remember hiding in the corner, sitting on my bed, anxious and afraid of my dad who was there and drunk and way too friendly. I learned to hide in the shower when he came into the bathroom time after time, month after month.

So, I learned to hide. And I got good at it. I got so good at it, that I could hide in a room full of people. Maybe they could see me, but they couldn't see the real me.

I also used my weight to hide. If I wasn't thin and attractive and didn't fuss with my hair and makeup, then people looked past me—not at me—and I could hide.

But at some point a few years ago, I realized that all this hiding was robbing me and my husband and my kids and my friends of the joy of knowing each other fully. God made me to be in relationship with others. But I couldn't do that if all I did was hide.

God is working in me and through me and healing me. I have seen him change things that I thought could never change. I've see Him use the hurt in my life to begin to heal others who have also been hurt.

As I have reached out to God, I have realized that He is a trustworthy father and that I don't have to hide from Him. And as I have reached out to others, I have found that, although they are not perfect, they can and do love me and want to see ME, even with all of my imperfections.

I found a verse in the Bible that makes me laugh, because after all of this learning and all of this growing, it tells me to hide. Colossians 3:3 says, "For you died to this life, and your real life is hidden with Christ in God." What a joy, what a relief—I am hidden and safe and comforted in Christ.

Britt Nicole sings a song that, if I didn't know better, I'd say was written about my life. The first part of *All This Time* says:

> *"I remember the moment, I remember the pain*
> *I was only a girl, but I grew up that day*
> *Tears were falling*
> *I know You saw me*
> *Hiding there in my bedroom, so alone*
> *I was doing my best, trying to be strong"*

But instead of moving on from there, I stayed, hiding. But the song goes on to say:

> *"All this time, from the first tear cried*
> *'Till today's sunrise*
> *And every single moment between*
> *You were there, You were always there*
> *It was You and I*
> *You've been walking with me all this time."*

Even if I don't get it, even if I wish the hurts had never happened, I am so glad to know God is with me and was with me and was loving me—even as I hid. And

He loved me so much, that He wouldn't let me stay there forever. For this I am grateful.

Anonymous Author

Joy In the Journey

I remember how excited I was to have my first "cattle call" audition. It was March 1992—two months before my college graduation. As much as I had thoroughly enjoyed college life, I couldn't wait to tackle the "real world." So off to Orlando I went to audition for a soprano spot in an a cappella vocal group that performed in Epcot in Disney World. At the conclusion of the first day, I was thrilled to find out that I had been chosen as one of the ten vocalists to return the next day for callbacks. The following morning, I woke up with absolutely no voice. I could not speak, let alone sing. What a frustration to have advanced that far in the process only to have it all come to a screeching halt due to an overnight onset of laryngitis. This wasn't the kind of "real world" I had anticipated.

Fast forward three months. A touring group based in Orlando (ironically) was looking for a female vocalist. Upon receiving my audition tape, a woman from the production company called. She informed me that as much as she was impressed with my tape, the position had unfortunately already been filled. Before she hung up the phone, she happened to ask how close I lived to a particular resort in West Virginia. I told her the resort was literally in my backyard. Upon hearing this, she requested that I come in for a live audition since that happened to be where the band was that very week. When she called the music director to have him arrange it, he informed her that one of the female vocalists had just told him that she was leaving the group. So I literally tried out on Thursday morning, packed all my stuff Thursday night, and started touring with the group Friday morning. It just so happened that that the drummer in the band would later become my husband. The crushing disappointment of not getting to sing for the Disney callback suddenly made sense. That door was basically slammed shut so that another door could open miraculously so I could meet the love of my life, John.

After having toured for a year and a half, John and I then worked as musicians for Princess Cruises prior to getting married. We were trying to decide where we would live after finishing our cruise contract. We were praying together and talking about the possibility of moving to Nashville since we both had an interest in getting involved with the Christian music industry. We asked God to give us confirmation if we were to move forward with those plans. The very next night, a woman approached us after we had finished one of our sets. "Have you ever considered moving to Nashville?" she asked. So one week after our wedding, we packed up what little we owned and moved to Nashville. We both began doing some session recording for songwriters pitching their songs to record labels. During that time we also became very involved with a church. We started volunteering with the worship team. I felt as if a deep passion had been awakened. I began to see how lives were changed as people drew closer to God when they worshiped God in song. What a privilege it was to be a part of helping others connect with God in a profound way. I started writing worship songs out of my desire to bring fresh expressions of prayers to God. Although my original intent was not to pursue a worship leader position, it became evident that it was where I found life and purpose.

Throughout my career as a vocalist/musician/worship leader, I have seen how disillusionment has been transformed into faith as I witness how circumstances rarely unfold as I envisioned them. As the years pass, the lessons learned along the path have become much more significant than reaching the final destination. The obstacles and trials that used to frustrate me have become tools used to shape me along the way. The older I become, the more I desire to live fully in the moment, invest in relationships, and receive all with a heart of gratitude. Knowing fully that I am loved by a God who created me to be in a relationship with Him and with others has freed me to be the woman I was crafted to be. My life has become an offering of worship to God instead of an attempt to prove my worth by accomplishing goals. The disappointments and failures have been used to bring wisdom and joy in the journey.

Jan L'Ecuyer

Choices

It was near the end of my four-year college degree and I was secretly dating the love of my life. Secretly, because I didn't have the guts to openly date a woman in the early 1980's. I was on top of the world. I had a small business, some cash in my pocket and a beautiful woman by my side. We were a fairy tale in the making, well, so I thought.

One day I came home from work early to find the love of my life passionately kissing someone in the driveway. Not just anyone, a friend of ours, a man! What?! This can't be happening! It's just a fluke. She's confused! She's just trying to figure things out. Or maybe she needs a father figure because this thug was old enough to be her dad?

As the days, weeks, and months passed, it was becoming increasingly clear that our relationship was over. I was crushed! All of this translated in my irrational, highly emotional brain that my life was over too. I was lost. I was lonely. We still ran in the same circle of friends and every time I saw her with him it was like ripping off a scab.

I thought about doing something drastic, like jumping down a muddy hill to cause injury to myself, not something serious enough to cause permanent damage, but enough to call attention to myself. Stupid, I know. But I would do anything to draw attention to myself to win her back. Oh, what was I thinking? Do I want someone like that back in my life anyway? As time passed, something became increasingly clear to me; I knew I had to get out of here. I needed to do something different with my life.

I made the decision to go back to school, and not just for my masters, but for my doctorate. I would immerse myself in school and that would consume every ounce of energy for at least a few years. So, that is what I did. I charted a new course for myself. I applied to eight schools, all out of state, that offered both the masters and doctorate programs combined. I was accepted into two, one in Kentucky and one in California. I immediately sold my business at a garage sale for $25,000 and headed west.

I used every dime I had to pay my way through school. I worked full-time and went to school full-time. Soon I didn't know anything different than eighteen-plus hours of working and studying, day after day after day, seven days a week. One night each week I would go country dancing so I could remember how to socialize with 'normal' people. But that was my only reprieve.

My plan worked. At the end of three very intense years, I graduated with my Doctorate in Industrial and Organizational Psychology. Mission accomplished. I no longer longed for my ex-lover. In fact, I only had her to thank for being the catalyst to a fabulous career. And, to top it off, I was engaged to be married, ironically, to a man.

I was not a fan of southern California so my fiancé and I moved to Colorado, half way between his family and mine. No friends, no jobs ... just Colorado. It was time to start searching for my career job. So, with the Ph.D. initials behind my name, I accepted a job at Taco

Bell. Yes, I know, fast food! Years later, I went to work for a consulting company, and then I eventually moved into HR work in the casino world. From there, I landed my career job working for Wells Fargo and now U.S. Bank. I am a Wealth Coach, I help families and teams understand who they are as individuals and how to be most effective in their communications. I make a difference in people's lives, one at a time.

It never ceases to amaze me how things come full circle, after ten years of existing in my marriage; I met my soul mate, an incredible woman. We have been together now for eleven years and I'm quick to brag, we have yet to have one argument.

In conclusion, it was my choice to go from emotional devastation to professional and relational success. I am on a path that is both emotionally and financially rewarding. My life is good! It was not an easy road or a short one, in fact it took about twenty years to come full circle, but it happened. And, it all came down to choices. It came down to having the courage to try new paths and start over, time and time again. Some people say I'm lucky because of what I have today. I say that I simply made the right choices.

Amy Zehnder

Moving Forward

As I stood alone in the tiny church bathroom, nervous hands gripping my sunflower bouquet, ankles shaky in unfamiliar heels, I took a moment to look at myself in the mirror one last time. On the surface, all appeared perfect; every twist of hair was curled and pinned in place, my white dress smooth and draped flawlessly. In mere minutes I'd walk down the aisle and take on a brand-new identity as a married woman, a wife. A few months of planning had ensured all the details—from the tuxes to the photographer to the banquet hall—were taken care of and ready-to-go. Waiting anxiously for my cue to enter the back of the church, however, I could not overlook the one painfully obvious component missing: my mom.

As a little girl conjuring up "Cinderella-esque" nuptials to an older, slightly more realistic young woman planning her wedding, I had always imagined my mother being highly involved in the process of my engagement. I envisioned us making appointments at bridal stores where she'd gush and fawn over every gown I tried on, finally breaking down when I walked out in *the dress*. I imagined her throwing my bridal shower, serving her famous chicken salad and sharing endearing stories from my childhood. Most importantly, though, she'd be with me at that crucial moment, holding my hand and steadying me as I took those first few steps into my new life.

Instead I waited alone. Somewhere deep down, I knew

my expectations had been far from realistic, but acceptance of my situation didn't make the hurt less strangling. It would be unfair to claim my mother was completely unattached, but she was never the consistently strong, positive role model I needed growing up as a girl. While my sisters and I attempted to survive the daily torture that was living with our father, my mother often hovered back in the shadows, watching vacantly as the stinging words fell, striking us down. She never took initiative, choosing instead to stay home and bend to the constantly changing will of her ever-demanding husband, even when that meant watching her children suffer right in front of her.

Growing up, there had been moments when I felt a true connection with my mother. I can remember times when I was home sick from school; she'd sneak away, bringing back coffee and donuts to enjoy while we watched silly daytime television. It was those precious few moments—the meaningful conservations, the soothing touches, the belly-aching laughs—that allowed me to glimpse the real woman my mother was; unfortunately, her true self was hidden behind a curtain of insecurity and fear. Waiting in that restroom, I yearned for my mom to be beside me, yet I knew her absence, at that moment, embodied so much of our real relationship. So, as the music began to beckon me forward, I walked myself to the back of the church and down the aisle to my future husband. Squeezing his hand, I didn't look back.

I suppose it's true that "time heals all broken hearts", but life can still feel overwhelming. Little moments catch me when I wish more than anything I could call my mom on the phone, asking for advice, for comfort, for strength. Thankfully, the gaps in my life my mother should have occupied have been filled by God to the point of overflowing. I have come to know and connect with the best female role models I ever could have imagined. Encouragement and love, from mother-in-law, aunts, and the amazing female staff at my pharmacy school, have helped transform me from a shy, reserved girl into a confident and self-empowered woman. These amazing role models know how to provide exactly what I need, at moments when I didn't realize I needed anything, and they never cease to amaze me with their sense of self and bigger sense of others. Daily, I am inspired by their generosity, humility, and passion for life.

The wounds are still healing, and while I never expect them to fully close over, it's comforting to know I am surrounded by women willing and able to lift me up and empower me to move forward. Blessed with such incredible mentors, I can only work to model myself after their example, and I know when the day comes, I'll be in that room with my own daughter, proud to have shown her the way.

Anonymous Author

Daddy's Little Girl

I grew up in the "normal" American family. There were four people in my family, living in a two-story house in a small town with a little beagle dog named Spanky. Both of my parents worked, but had schedules where they were mostly home with us. We went to church every Sunday and from an early age my Christian beliefs were instilled and important to me. I was baptized at the age of nine and have been attending the same church since that time.

I was daddy's little girl and could do no wrong in his eyes! But, at the age of fifteen, all this changed. It was July 25, 1989 and dad had been complaining of a "pulled muscle" in his shoulder for a few weeks. Mom pushed him to going to see his doctor, which led to an x-ray where a tumor was found. It was lung cancer and within two weeks we found that it was inoperable. The cancer had possibly metastasized from another primary spot in his body and chemotherapy was unlikely to help. We quickly went into "full-press court" mode and took dad to Cleveland for a second opinion. He was placed on an investigational drug that required my mom to take him to Cleveland five days a week. This treatment lasted just shy of six weeks and we received more bad news—it was not working and palliative care/hospice was his only option. Dad stayed at our home for the remainder of his life ... and died just six months after his diagnosis.

This tragic time was a pivotal moment in my life. It could have either destroyed me or defined me; I chose the latter. I reached more for my relationship with Christ and He carried me through this time. It was not easy and there were times when I questioned everything in my life. My brother had left for college the fall after dad passed away, which left mom and I to pick up the pieces, in many ways, alone. We did most things together and for the next few years she was both the mother and "father" figure in my life.

Two years later I went off to college to get my pharmacy degree. I was struggling and felt like I needed to follow my brother; after all he was my only family male role model. So I followed in my older brother's footsteps and attended Ohio Northern University. Truth be told, this was because I knew I would be terribly home sick and he would be there! In my first year of graduate school, I experienced another life-changing moment when I met my future husband, Mike. We had a long-term relationship for the next year and half and fell in love with one another. He just "got me" from the beginning and fit well into my family. In many ways, Mike had and still has similar traits to that of my father. We got engaged in my final year of graduate school and married in 1999, almost three years after meeting!

Looking back over the last twenty-three years, I see how my relationships with my mother, brother, extended family and friends have evolved and changed since the passing of my dad. As for mom and I, we are more like friends and have helped each other in the good, bad and ugly times. There have been times where she acts like and advises me as a mother, and other times when I have done that for her. My brother and I have a great relationship, but it's been tough. I am a talker and feel comfort in openly discussing memories of dad, where my brother prefers not to talk about him. He struggles with why God allowed this tragedy to happen to our family. However, he has always been that "male figure" in my life. My brother came home from college to take pictures of my prom and harassed my date. He walked me down the aisle and was the first one to see me after the birth of my first child. My extended family sees me as the "rock" of my family. It's kind of funny, as I often feel personally like the one who questions it most and yet, they always tell me how proud they are of me for persevering during those difficult times and coming out on top! The uncles and male cousins in my life are all special and I find great comfort in them and the roles they have played in my life as well.

Today, being a mother of three children, I realize how important the "father figure" is to a young child. I understand this due to the relationship my husband has with the children and the way he positively fills this role. After all, girls are attracted to guys like their father! My relationship with my husband has helped fill this void in my life and I find such great joy in watching my daughters interact with their daddy just like I did with mine.

People often ask me, when they hear that I lost a parent early in my life, if I feel as though I missed out? That's a tough question because the obvious answer is yes! I got the short end of the stick when it came to a lifelong relationship with my father, however, the longer answer is that I was blessed to have been his daughter for just over sixteen years and the impact he made on my life in that short time was so powerful. I still remember scents that he had, songs he liked to sing and foods he liked to eat. I remember his facial expressions and his excitement when my brother or I would win a game in tee ball! I am able to say this also because I have had a Heavenly Father who has been able to fill this void of sadness in many ways. He has carried me when needed and provided so many blessings in my life, for that, I am forever grateful and know that soon, I will join my earthly father again in a much better place!

Michelle Cudnik

Thank You, Cancer!

My world changed on April 16, 2007. I was a few hours away from a weeklong vacation and was busy at work checking items off of my "to do" list so my mind would be free while I was away. I remember the day like it was yesterday. It was raining outside; the spring air was a bit gloomy. It was approximately 2:00PM when the phone rang and her voice was crystal clear. My surgeon called immediately upon review of my biopsy results to tell me that I had breast cancer. Yep, thirty-one years old, five days before my birthday, I was delivered the most *significant* news of my entire life. I planned to go to my sister's house that night to celebrate my birthday. Oh, I went to her house anyway, but the event was far from a birthday party. We sat on the couch and cried. And cried. And a few moments later, I said, "It's okay. Somehow I knew this was meant to be".

I cannot explain how I knew breast cancer was going to be an important part of my life, but I remember distinct moments when there were connections to breast cancer that caused me to pause and reflect. My first memory of breast cancer was as a five year old when a loving neighbor was diagnosed. I was ridiculously afraid of learning about chemotherapy and oncology topics in pharmacy school. As a pharmacy resident, one of my first teaching assignments was breast cancer screening. As a frugal resident, I was invited to a home party for a popular line of baskets where I felt compelled to buy a specific basket because the proceeds were donated to breast cancer research. Sure, these could be random acts that I am tying together, but I wish you could experience the commentary going on in my psyche. There was something personal and significant about each of these events and many others I haven't mentioned. On April 16, 2007, literally hours after I received the news, I felt a sense of relief. It finally made sense.

Overall, my experience with cancer was very positive. My treatment included surgery and chemotherapy. My surgeries were uncomplicated. The chemotherapy included relatively mild and tolerable adverse effects. Losing my hair was devastating, but the convenience of a stylish wig was awesome! One month and one day after my diagnosis, my thirty-five year old sister was diagnosed. She had no reason to go in for evaluation, except for my diagnosis. Perhaps my diagnosis saved her life? Her experience was also very positive. Together, we are committed to sharing our positive experiences with other women. One goal is to combat the negative connotations surrounding the word 'cancer'. More importantly, we share our stories because the experience changed our lives for the BETTER.

Before cancer, I was an accomplished professional, willing to spend work time and a significant amount of my personal time completing work-related activities; mostly because I love my profession and the day-to-day work that I do. I would make time for fun, but I enjoyed working hard and I knew that "someday" I would have the luxury of putting less effort into my professional life to further develop my personal life. After cancer, I accomplished more professionally and spent less personal time committed to work-related activities. For real? Yes.

Cancer made me a better professional? Yes. But in reality, cancer made me a better person.

When you are faced with your own mortality, suddenly life is put into perspective ... crystal clear perspective. At thirty years old, my own death was far from my mind. Death is for old people. Yet suddenly that was all I could think about. Who I am? What does life mean to me? Am I ready to die? Am I really living life to the fullest? What do I wish to accomplish in this life? What a transformation that was triggered by that fateful day. Through self-reflection, I am grateful that cancer chose me and changed my life at such an early age. I am so lucky to realize at age thirty-two the meaning of life and the importance of happiness! I learned the importance of living a wholesome and well-rounded life long before my life on this earth ends, thereby giving me many years to truly live! I am grateful for the physical and emotional scars that remind me every day of these important lessons.

Professionally, cancer helps me to be a better teacher, leader and manager. I strive to instill important life lessons in my students through my experiences. I share my story with them, not only as a cancer survivor, but also as a pharmacist who learned important lessons as a patient. If my personal journey inspires one student to become a more caring and compassionate pharmacist without having to go through a similar experience, then I have made a difference. As a leader of a large department, I also feel a level of personal responsibility for the many faculty and staff who report to me. Our department has substantial responsibilities that contribute toward the mission of our college and university.

This requires those reporting to me to work hard and accomplish important goals. I am blessed with a group of high achieving, dedicated, hard working individuals who certainly give their blood, sweat, and tears to the work I ask them to do. You know what? I also tell them to stop working and go home, to spend time with their families, to take care of their own health and wellness. Yes, I am a boss and I said that I tell people to stop working. Through my experience, I learned the importance of balance in life; of being fulfilled through multiple facets of one's existence. And guess what? The more I encourage my employees to focus on their overall well-being, the more we get to experience great accomplishments together. Of course I am proud of the important work accomplished by my team. But more importantly, I am grateful that my experience indirectly influences each and every one of them to become well rounded and successful, personally and professionally.

Every time I reflect on my experience with breast cancer, I cannot help but say thank you to the universe for giving me this life-changing experience. Until recently, April 16th was a day of tears and joy. This last April, I celebrated my sixth anniversary as a cancer survivor. It was the first year I actually faced the people in my day-to-day life and didn't cry. This doesn't mean this day is any less significant or emotional for me. In fact, April 16th has truly become an annual celebration of life, wellness and happiness. Thank you, cancer, for making a transformational, positive difference in my life!

Susan Bruce

When Life Does Not Go According to Plan

In the summer of 2004, my husband and I decided to try for a baby. We had stable jobs and a brand new home. We lived in sunny Florida with two cats and enjoyed simple times. That fall, we had a few hurricanes and we actually had to evacuate. Thankfully nothing of ours was damaged or lost. Despite hurricane chaos we soon found out we were pregnant! Everything progressed well until the spring of 2005. My dad was complaining of not feeling well lately and had seen a doctor a few times. He always downplayed his symptoms and continued to work long hours as a pharmacist. We had a special baby shower planned with my family in Atlanta the same day as my dad's 58th birthday, April 24th. I was so excited to show everyone my ultrasound pictures of our new baby boy! He was the first boy to be born on my side of the family in eighty years and he was the first grandchild on my side as well. To have the opportunity to celebrate with my Atlanta family was just "the icing on the cake". In fact, that was the only time I've ever had all of my side of the family, with the exception of my grandpa who was out of the country, under one roof.

The day came and we were excited! The guests arrived and my dad was late, as usual. When he finally did arrive, I knew something was really wrong. Everyone could tell. In fact, he was only fifty-eight but looked like an eighty year old man. He was in terrible pain and I was completely caught off guard by his appearance. We progressed through the party and were blessed by the love and support from everyone who attended. I hugged my dad and begged him to go to the hospital. He declined. It was an awful day to be blindsided by his obvious sickness and yet it was a tremendous day to be blessed and loved on by my extended family.

We returned to Florida and went back to planning for our baby to arrive that July. Yes, pregnant in July, in Florida. Fun? The very next day my aunt and uncle forced my dad to go to the E.R. It turned out he was very, very sick with cancer in his colon and liver. It was inoperable and he was probably not going to leave the hospital alive. In fact, his oncologist said to me, "I can't believe your dad walked into the hospital on his own". That's my stubborn but loveable dad! The next two weeks were a blur as he received treatments and a terminal diagnosis. We spoke our last words to each other over the phone. Thankfully, I was at least able to say "goodbye," if that is even possible with someone so important in your life. He died two weeks later on Mother's Day; my first Mother's Day. My husband was the one to take the phone call and had to tell me. We buried him on a Wednesday. It was sunny and hot and very hard to do. I'm an only child and had the full financial responsibility to handle everything. I was seven and a half months pregnant and wanted nothing more than for my dad to get to see his first grandchild; a grandson, before he died. It felt as if God took him before that could happen. I was confused why a God, who is supposed to be so good, would do something so painful to me.

My days and weeks after his funeral were spent

cleaning his very dirty house and settling his disorganized estate. My husband had to quit his job in order to be available for appointments in Georgia as I was no longer allowed to travel. My job was minimized also as I approached maternity leave and could not handle full time work outside in the Florida heat. Our finances were tight and would only get tighter. Hurricane Dennis came when I was 38 weeks pregnant. We evacuated our home due to hurricane threats. Ugh. Why was all this happening to me when I was supposed to have this safe and easy pregnancy? Finally the day came when Ben was born. He was healthy and beautiful. He was my ray of sunshine in the midst of paying double bills on two homes and grieving the loss of my dad. It was like my husband and I were in survival mode as we tackled the next hurdle of paying off my dad's debt, hiring an attorney out of state, putting my dad's house up for sale (the house I grew up in) all while learning how to be parents. And then Hurricane Katrina came. Thankfully we were not in her path and were minimally affected by the food and gasoline shortages. A life of hurricane anxiety was not the life I wanted to live with my new baby! Within the next year we sold both our house and my dad's house, moved 1,000 miles, bought a new house near family up north and my husband got a new job. He had been off for our first seven months as parents and was a great support to me. I firmly believe his presence helped to prevent any postpartum depression that could have occurred.

During this time I struggled in my faith, something that had always come easy for me. I leaned heavily on the two books by Stormie O'Martian called, "The Power of a Praying Woman" and "The Power of a Praying Wife".

I grasped at God's promises in His word that His plans are good for me despite the very scary storms we face in life. I learned that sometimes there just isn't an answer for why God allows some things to happen. I learned to release my "control" of always having an answer and learned to trust that somehow, some way, God would use it for good and would bring healing; but the answers we seek might not come until heaven. For a long time it was difficult for me to see other daughters with their dads. It was hard to attend a wedding and see the bride dance with her father.

One very special blessing came out of this loss. I had prayed that I could be a stay at home mom. Considering our finances while we were expecting, this may as well have been asking for the moon. But, through losing my dad and gaining a modest inheritance, I was blessed to be able to be a stay at home mom. It came at a high price but I will always be grateful for that last "gift" my dad gave me.

Now that I am a parent, this experience has shaped my approach to my children; to be much more patient and considerate. I do not consider myself to be a patient person but as the memories of my dad come to mind, I cherish the fact that he modeled patience to me. He was an "in the moment" kind of parent and I want to be that person too. He was always cheerful and rarely if ever said unkind words when he certainly had grounds to lash out. It sounds cliché to say we never know when someone is going to be taken from us, but it really is true. I am making a point to make sure those memories my family and children have of me are ones they will value and grow from as well. In fact, I wonder, if he had not died, if I would have paid as much attention to his kindness to me or just taken it for granted.

The following summer I attended a grieving support group at my local church. While arduous to attend, it worked God's healing into deep places in my heart, specifically my memory. See, I have a good memory and I'm the kind of person who can remember how someone hurt me for a long time. In this group, I learned that I can "be bitter or be better". I can be bitter that life is most certainly not fair and that God seemed silent during those hard times. Or, I can be a better person and release the sour stench that unforgiveness and bitterness brings. I can be bitter about what I felt I lost or I can be grateful for the time I did have with my dad and choose to bless my own children with those same special memories. Even now, years later, it is a daily choice. The pain of loss never completely goes away although the days and nights do get easier. I believe God is an amazing Healer who comforts the broken hearted and loves us beyond what we can imagine. I believe He values our relationship with Him more than He values our comfort/happiness and He will use anything it takes to draw us to His side. But, when we press in, when we surrender and when we forgive, He truly gives peace to our soul beyond what our mind knows. I would challenge you, when life does not go according to plan, to go to God instead of turning from Him. Ask Him what His plan is and ask for His perspective to see the situation as He sees it. He cares for us endlessly and one day we will get to be back in our father's arms, forever.

Julia Lawson

My "Wee Pea"

Growing up female meant a fine balance between the expectations of a girl growing up in a very conservative Christian home and being drawn to the areas of science and math. My father was a math teacher and my mother had been a math teacher prior to having me. Both were always supportive of my desire to pursue a career in the sciences but even from an early age, I was always told at home there were "girl jobs" and "boy jobs." Being the oldest of four children and my only sister being eleven years younger than me, this meant a lot of work around the house. I did not mind too much and especially liked the fact I was not expected to do much yard work.

Additionally, I lived a fairly sheltered life. We went to church three times a week and I did not get into much trouble. Was I strong-willed? Yes. Was I sometimes rebellious? Yes, but I never did anything crazy. I was too scared of my grandparents and parents to do anything too wild. I graduated number one in my high school class and went on to a private church affiliated school in the south. Between curfew, nightly "bed checks", and a long laundry list of rules (which my father loved), I accepted and respected the whole process. I was majoring in Biochemistry, heading for pharmacy school, and having the time of my life all while securing my future by meeting my husband-to-be.

Fast forward through pharmacy school, my husband's medical school and both of our residencies. I was a successful pediatric clinical pharmacist. My husband had just finished his internal medicine residency and was going to practice a year as a hospitalist while waiting to pursue an infectious diseases fellowship. The timing was perfect. Time to have the family I had always dreamed of. Coming from a conservative Christian background, many families we associated with had several children and many women either worked part-time or not at all. I was the strange one who had a career as successful as my husband's but now was my time to do my most important job and become a mom. I had been collecting activities to do with our future children for years. I had children's place settings for my silverware and china pattern and decorative cake pans for future birthday parties. I could not wait to do all of these cool kid things but unfortunately, this was not going to be the easy process it had been for the vast majority of people around me.

The first year we didn't get pregnant, we simply thought we had not given it enough time. The next six months we tried everything including basal thermometers and ovulation test kits. After eighteen months with no little one in sight, I started to get worried. Had I waited too long to start a family? Had we put our careers ahead of a future family and waited for the timing to be what we considered "right"? At this point, I decided to go to my internist to ask some tough questions. She drew blood work and everything appeared normal but still referred my husband and I to an infertility clinic.

Our first visit to the infertility clinic was a scary one! We did not know what to expect and we both had strong opinions about the beginning of a life. We had more tests and the results indicated that a few minor areas could be adjusted but nothing major was found. After that initial visit, I looked over all of the materials the clinic presented. You would never believe all of the different options available to couples to have a child. I thought long and hard about what I personally could and could not do. Obviously, you start with the least invasive practices first and work your way to the top depending on your circumstances. I decided there were certain things I could not do; the biggest one being *in vitro* fertilization (IVF). I knew people who had undergone IVF and knew the ups and downs of the procedure. I am not morally opposed to it; it was simply not something I thought I could tackle. Because I am a pediatric pharmacist, I saw the struggles of those who underwent IVF and had babies who required care in the neonatal intensive care unit (NICU). I also struggled with what I would do with potential embryos that were not implanted and remained in limbo awaiting a decision. I think coming to a realization of what I could and could not live with and discussing this with my husband was the most important step I made. Did I struggle with the thought of never having a child if it came to this? Yes, but throughout the process I was resolved to a certain course, even if it meant no child. My husband and I agreed if it did not work, we would adopt. There are plenty of children in this world who need the love of two caring people.

We decided to go on the trip of a lifetime before starting the first round of infertility medication. We now fondly call this our "pity party for not having a child yet". We had the time of our lives and I think it helped recharge both of us before we tackled this issue. The first round of infertility medication was oral clomiphene. I have never been so "hormonal" in all my life. It was five days of weeping like I had never wept before. The slightest thing would set me off. In addition to the hormones, my husband and I were scared and a little embarrassed by the whole process so we told no one except my mother what we were doing. I could not handle everyone staring at me to see if I got pregnant. I had already endured that annoying question of "When are you going to have a baby?" for the last several years. Then the most disappointing news came, my follicles were not big enough and they wanted me to continue with another five days of clomiphene at twice the dose I was currently taking. I was at my breaking point but I pulled myself together and took five more days of clomiphene. After another five days of the hormonal roller coaster I finally had two follicles big enough for intrauterine insemination (IUI).

After the IUI procedure, the waiting game began. Would something happen? Would I get pregnant? I prayed like I had never prayed before. I asked God for a miracle, and He answered. Two weeks after my IUI, I took my first pregnancy test. It was the longest three minutes of my life. The test was positive! I was ecstatic when I was able to confirm the over-the-counter test results with blood results at the clinic. I was so over the moon I actually wrecked the car in the hospital parking lot; an event I later found out happens to many pregnant women. However, I knew this was not a done deal. I had friends who had suffered early losses of pregnancies and others who had suffered as far out as the second trimester. I wanted to be extra careful. We only told our parents and one of my closest friends. An ultrasound in two weeks would confirm the pregnancy. The first time

I saw my son on that ultrasound screen I fell in love. The heartbeat was the most precious sound I had ever heard. This was the first time I had ever seen my husband become emotional. The second would be at the birth of our son. I cherish that first ultrasound picture of our little "wee pea," which affectionately became our son's nickname.

We had our ups and downs of pregnancy. At thirteen weeks I told everyone I was pregnant and then was faced with a vaginal bleeding scare. Otherwise, I had a fairly smooth pregnancy, a rather "quick" delivery, and a rough first eight weeks with my newborn son. Despite all that, nothing compares to the joy I have each night when I kiss him goodnight. He is our "Gift from God" as his middle name, Matthew, reaffirms. I would move heaven and earth for him. There is no doubt in my mind that I would defend him to the death if called to do so.

Our story does not end there. When our son was eighteen months old, we thought about having a second child. We knew couples that said conception of a second child was much easier since the pressure to have the first child was off. We wanted a bigger family so we sought out an infertility clinic and again our chances were still not great. We were told we had hit the jackpot by getting pregnant during our first round of clomiphene, reaffirming our belief he was truly a miracle from God.

Again, we started with infertility medicine but this time, six times without success. This was heart wrenching for me. I saw every time as a failure on my part. Additionally, at the end of the sixth failed attempt, my father passed away from an aggressive cancer that claimed his life only ten short weeks after his diagnosis. I realized my father would never see my son grow up and now would not be there if I did have a second child. We took a break from the process and decided to take things a bit slower. We explored super-ovulation and eventually over the course of a year tried three rounds without success. At this point, we were at the final step, IVF. Would I do it? We decided not to. We were blessed with one son and have considered adoption as an option in the future. We decided to concentrate on the family we already had. We feel blessed with the joys of a son who, without a shadow of a doubt, was sent by God to not only try my patience but also be the most precious gift I could ever receive.

I have grown closer in my faith and my family through this experience. Ironically, though another benefit has been education to students and fellow colleagues. The opportunity came for me to teach several classes on women's health at the college of pharmacy at which I am currently a faculty member. I took the infertility lectures without question. The first time I taught I did not express much of my own experiences because it was a big class and I was still a bit shy about my personal struggles. However, when I later went on to share my experiences in a small group setting of students in a women's health elective, I have never known a more therapeutic experience. This gave me the courage to share my story and experiences with several colleagues and larger groups of students as well. The following year, I taught with much more feeling and emotion. I explained the personal aspects of the condition and how it can affect one's life. I shared the sad fact that most likely at least one person in this class would go through the same struggles as my family. In the end, I hope my experiences can help those around me. We do not know what is planned for us. Some people do not struggle at all to have children while others go through fertility treatments without success. However, I have learned that it is the amount of love between the members, not the number of the people that makes an incredible family.

M. Petrea Cober

Life's Trials Build Character

We all have heard the sayings, 'What doesn't kill us makes us stronger' and 'God only gives us what we can handle'. For most of us these are just sayings, but I have firsthand experience that these are very true. I was in my mid-thirties when my world changed. All at once my father, mother and father-in-law were in the hospital for various health issues. My husband had his brother and sister to support him, but as an only child, I was dealing with my parents illnesses on my own. I was forced to face the mortality of my parents and with that, their faults. Even as an adult I still viewed my parents with the same child like eyes I did during my childhood. It was very difficult to see my parents as fallible humans when I had viewed them as heroes who could do no wrong in my eyes.

My father was as stubborn as an ox and was fighting to keep living. My mother, on the other hand, was passive and more accepting of her fate. My father had CPR performed and was put on a ventilator more than five times in five months. He had severe chronic pulmonary disease and emphysema from years of being a heavy smoker. He could barely get a few words out before stopping to catch his breath, but was determined to go home from the hospital every time. During one visit, after being weaned from the ventilator, my husband and I discussed with my father that his constant CPR saves and ventilator dependence were doing more harm than good. However, my father wanted every means possible in place to preserve his life, which included feeding tubes and remaining on mechanical ventilation. After heart wrenching conversations with my father, it became clear to my husband and I that he was scared to die from not being able to breathe and thought all of these interventions would prevent death by suffocation. The look in my father's eyes was as if he had an "ah ha" moment when we explained to him all of this medical treatment would not help with that. The reality was staring him in the face. Part of me was relieved, since his body had taken such abuse from the years of smoking and the multiple life resuscitation attempts. The other part of me was scared for him. He looked so child-like and the reality of his situation was also staring me in the face. Denial can be a very helpful coping mechanism, but the truth will always win out in the end. When he finally accepted his fate, you could see the weight had been lifted from his shoulders and he had the knowledge he needed ... to know he was still in control of his own fate. We were able to say our 'I love yous' and felt as if we were in a good place. I remember walking into his hospital room (after he had passed away) and seeing a look of peace on his face that I hadn't seen before. I knew he had died on his own terms and was finally home.

Since my mother was also in the hospital dealing with her congestive heart issues the same week my father passed away, I had to alter my mentality in dealing with her since she was more passive than my father. She was fine letting me handle all of my father's final arrangements, selling my childhood home and helping her recover. At this point, our roles had reversed and she had become the child and I the parent. After nine long months of rehab, she was finally able to live on her own and I found her an apartment that would accommodate her needs due to her physical limitations. Mom lived on her own for six months before her congestive heart failure caused her to go back in the hospital and eventually rehab again. At this point I could see she was getting more passive and the reality of living on her own was not what she had originally envisioned. She had dreams of what her 'golden years' would be like and they didn't include being a widow with a chronic illness. During her last hospital stay, the doctors told us that her kidneys were starting to fail. They suggested dialysis and mom fiercely refused. This objection was the most assertive she had been during her whole illness. The idea of being hooked up to a machine to live was more than she could imagine. Later that day she asked me point blank, "When am I going to die?"' I was shocked and thought, "How do you answer that question especially when it's your own parent?" I tried to make the situation as light as possible and stated that the timing wasn't for us to decide. That night as my husband and I snuck out of her room to go home, she said, "Take care you two."' in a strong clear voice. That was the last time I heard my mother's voice. She had never regained consciousness and my husband and I camped out in her palliative care room at the hospital for her last few days. I talked to her as if she was awake, saying I love you and that it was ok to go 'home'. On that last day it was just she and I when she took her last breath; just as it was when I took my first breath.

The death of my parents and the events surrounding it all happened within an eighteen month timeframe. I spent many days and nights, during that time and in the five years since, reliving these events and others of my past. I can recall numerous times I've stopped and asked the infamous question, 'Why?' every time thinking why didn't I do this, or I shouldn't have done that, or maybe if I said this things would have been different. I can remember thinking, "I can't take another step, another breath or deal with one more thing. What did I do to deserve this? What am I supposed to learn?" One can be consumed with the would of, could of, and should of a situation when reflecting back on things. After six months of grief counseling and a lot of introspection, I realized that I could continue to dwell on all the difficulties, heartaches, and fears that would make me a miserable person, or I could become a stronger, wiser, and more compassionate person. I chose the latter. We don't know what God's big picture for us is, but He knows what is best and what we are able to endure. His plan is definitely not for us to question or doubt. Through these trials in our life, our true character is built, and the lesson learned from those trials is that we have no control over other people or the events in our life, but we do have control of how we choose to react to them.

Nora Helscel

When Your Life Hits a Brick Wall

I was the perfect little blonde girl. I felt I grew up in an absolutely "normal' family. I hardly ever got in trouble. I got spanked only once that I remember. Of course I had the occasional fights with my brother, but that was to be expected. I went to a good school, was loved by my family, had a lot of friends, got good grades, and was a star athlete. My parents loved and supported both my brother and I and were exceptional role models. They still snuggle on the couch and hold hands to this day. There were few if any arguments in the family home. Yes, you could say I lived the life of a golden child.

I never remember spending a lot of time with my dad when I was younger. It was always girls with the girls and boys with the boys. Therefore, any special attention I got from my dad was treasured. I remember he brought me a treasured *Holly Hobby* purse home from Chicago. I am surprised I still don't have it to this day. I used to pretend I liked scary movies so I could watch them with my dad because it was just the two of us. My brother was always too scared and cowered in the bedroom. I really didn't like the movies but it was my chance to be with my dad. (Horror movies are not my first choice to this day.) He coached my baseball team, which have to be some of my absolute best memories. He believed our team could do anything even though every year we were the worst team in the league. Once he gave us a speech and had us so fired up we won an impossible game and finished in second place that year. He believed in us like no other coach I have ever had. He talks about me now as a young baseball player and I swear he gets a sparkle in his eye.

My mom and I were inseparable at this time. There was really no one I would rather be with when I was younger; that is at least until I was a teenager. I hated when she left us to go to work. I had, what I called, that "end of the world feeling" in my stomach. I think now it would be correctly labeled as anxiety. I really never liked to stay overnight at a friend's because I became anxious being away from her. One time I was at a friend's house for a sleep over and I called her and made her come get me. She wondered why but I never really remember having the words to explain how I felt. She was my shopping buddy, my confidante, my teacher, and honestly, my best friend.

I do not recall having emotional feelings as I was growing up or remember being able to verbalize them. I never remember anyone talking about feelings in my family. I remember thinking it was bad to have anxiety or be sad about things. At my grandmother's funeral I was asked why my eyes were red? Was I not supposed to cry? We lived in the glass house. I never witnessed my parents fighting and never a raised voice between them. If the girls got crabby the boys blamed it on PMS and took off in the fishing boat. My mom screamed on very rare occasions; usually at my brother for not cleaning up his room. Of course, there were the few teenage disturbances between children and their parents, but for the most part everyone was pretty much agreeable. I had the ingrained Catholic conscience that would never permit lying to your parents. I kid you not there were nights when I crept down to their bedroom to confess before I could go to sleep in peace.

But that was growing up and somewhere in between there and here my life hit the brick wall (or so I like to say). I took the well-travelled road of a college graduate, got married and ended up in the most mentally devastating predicament I could ever have imagined. As a result of knowing only my safe haven as a child, I arrived with ineffective coping skills and inept at battling against an emotionally abusive husband. Who knew what boundaries were, how to protect yourself, and when to take a stand against a bully? These were things I never had to do growing up. As a result, I crawled into a deep dark place to protect myself and withdrew from the world around me. Through many years of counseling and the love of my family I managed to recover from the trenches of the battlefield I like to refer to as my marriage.

I used to wonder, "Where will I end up?" I don't know that I will ever really have that answer. Just when you think you know where you are going, you hit a bump in the road. It is baffling to me, even to this day, to think I have it all under control and then still get thrown off my well-planned course. I often wonder how many times I have to learn the same lesson over and over before I get it right. But as the wise teachers say, "Repeat, repeat, repeat and it is only then that you will really learn."

I continue to make "mistakes" in my newfound world. I still, at times, think they are catastrophic, but, I now know there are people around me supporting me and helping me to see it is not about the "mistake" but the bigger lessons we learn during these times. It would be impossible never to blunder. It is impossible to expect yourself to be perfect since life's paths ahead of you are new and you don't get to practice before trying them. You just do the best you can with what you have at the time. I have learned there is no longer any punishment, only love and support coming from women who are just like me, surrounding me everyday.

Over the years of struggle and triumph what have I learned? Here it goes. There is no way to predict what will happen in the future and therefore no need to let mistakes break you down when you fail to live life perfectly. Your mistakes do not define you and just maybe they are not really mistakes. As you get some experience under your belt you learn to accept them for what they are—lessons learned. They will no longer take you down your old slippery slope. I think these were the tools I was lacking before—the insight and the ability to reflect and see the bigger picture. The true value in living one's life comes from taking these lessons and storing them away in your knowledge bank of wisdom.

People often say they are thankful for the rocky road they have been led down because it allowed them to be the person they have become. As I sit here today, I can honestly say it has been one hell of a ride but not one I would have changed. Okay, maybe I would have changed a few things. It was so hard at times I honestly thought I would have rather been dead. Somehow I managed to walk away from a place of darkness and towards a brighter future. Maybe it has been more like a crawl, but nonetheless not all at once and certainly still a work in progress. Now I look back at that brick wall as my opportunity to find my own path and in essence maybe I have finally become myself.

Stacey Schneider

Who Am I, Really?

I've always been a glass-half-full kind of gal. You know, all Pollyanna with a positive outlook on life. I'd like to think I'm an eternal optimist of sorts. I've been an encourager and personal cheerleader for my family and so many friends over the years. So why then do I constantly look back at my past and feel self-defeat?

I've looked back at the situations I've experienced in life and more times than not, the negative ones jump to the front of the line, ahead of the positive ones. Yes, I've endured my share of unpleasant experiences in life. However, why do we seem to define ourselves by our negative experiences instead of viewing ourselves through a positive lens? It would seem that the perception of my own life is mimicking that of a glass half empty, or else I'm focusing on being a negative Nellie who sees everything that's been wrong or bad in my world.

First of all, misery loves company. We all have the proverbial skeleton in our closet, albeit personal mistakes or those we have been lumped into by association. Guess what? So does every other woman on this planet. Heck, even Eve could look back and dwell on the fact that she ate the forbidden fruit. And thus, women have been dwelling on our former mishaps ever since. I suppose since every woman has difficult experiences in her story, she can do one of two things: she can define herself by her negative past circumstances, or she can define herself by the ambition of the promise of her positive future.

Secondly, we women compare ourselves to each other in every category of life. We concern ourselves with our physical appearances, our mothering skills, our past experiences, our career choices, and our ability to decorate our houses. However, in the midst of all those moments that just don't seem to measure up, there are always memorable occasions that exceeded our expectations and continue to stand out as defining moments in our lives. Those should be the focus points to which we should springboard down the path of our futures filled with hope. Who really cares whether or not your table centerpiece is a gluey creation from your three year old or an expensive glitter-clad Martha Stewart original? What matters most is that you and your family are happy and your days are filled with joy; not whether you're a stay-at-home mother or a successful CEO for a million dollar corporation.

You know what? I've realized I've been an actress way too long. My mask almost seems like a permanent piece of my wardrobe; an extension of my personality and character. Today, I am taking off the mask. I am not going to hide or cover up any longer because I'm afraid of what people will think. God uses our experiences to help others. Maybe THAT is why I keep looking back? Those experiences are my connective points to others who have lived through life situations similar to mine. However, rather than saying I was divorced, a victim of childhood sexual abuse, suffered through a spousal affair, endured not one but BOTH of my babies being admitted to neonatal intensive care, and was a people-pleaser to the fault of emotional anxiety ... I am choosing to see myself by my positive accomplishments and experiences. I am learning to look through to the top of my half-full glass of life. I am fortunate to have *earned a bachelor's degree*. I have been *happily married* for sixteen years. I am a *survivor* of childhood sexual abuse. I have *two beautiful, healthy children*. I have *learned to say no* with confidence and freedom. But most of all, I am proud to say *I am a child of God*. He originally thought of me. He created me. He has a great plan for my life, despite all I've endured. God pulled me through the muck and mire and is now using my life experiences to help others. I am able to give women hope because I made it through the trenches, put the pieces back together, have been healed emotionally, spiritually, physically, and can finally remove my mask with confidence.

Finally, I recognize that my life didn't unfold as I had originally imagined or expected. There were times when my glass was almost empty and nearly dry. But God poured His living water into my soul and filled me up. Today I am able to share my refreshing story because my glass is now overflowing with love, acceptance and grace. Will I ever forget about those not-so-perfect times in my life? No. However, like a scar from a terrible wound, I am often reminded of those painful experiences. But as time goes by and I allow my character to be developed through my situations, those imperfect times simply become memories of things that happened to me. Those moments don't necessarily hurt me anymore, and I know now, they certainly don't indicate who I am or am not.

So, who am I? What you see is what you get. I am Lori!

Lori Bodkin

Epilogue... Extraordinary Destinations

You choose every day how to embrace the gift of the day you've been given. So what are you going to do? Will you choose to dwell in the sorrows of your mayhem and mishaps? Or will you enthusiastically accept the challenge to lunge forward unapologetically in this adventure called life and seize the day with all its perfect and imperfect moments? I believe all of our glasses are half full and you can choose to fill it or spill it every single day for the rest of your life. Indulge and quench the thirst you've been holding yourself back to enjoy. Be refreshed in the spirit of life that surrounds you day after day. Who knows, maybe your renewed outlook will spill over on another woman who just might need a splash of encouragement to set her foot on the right path—the path to becoming herself.

Stacey and I want to thank all of the marvelous women who allowed us to share their stories. Each one we read and edited made us laugh and cry and reminded us how very blessed we are to be surrounded by truly magnificent women. There are so many inspiring stories and life lessons within these pages. We hope you were inspired as well and will take away your own bits and pieces and apply the lessons to your own life story.

So here's to you, a woman with an ordinary beginning, taking a look at her journey through life's ups, downs, and sideways experiences. You are only a short step away from your extraordinary destination; from developing into a beautiful pearl. Embrace all the perfect and imperfect moments that have brought you to this place; a place where you become all you were designed to be ... a simply amazing woman!

Lori

Questions for Discussion

- What is the significance of the title? Would you have titled it something different? If yes, what would you use as your title?

- What story most resonated with you personally either in a positive or negative way?

- Has anything ever happened to you similar to what happened to any of the authors in the book?

- What is different about the perspective from the beginning stories and the ending stories?

- Why do you think the experienced women titled their stories?

- Is there a common theme you see in all of these stories?

- Do you think there is specific character trait that helps women as they mature and experience life?

- Do you think there is a specific character trait that hinders women as they mature and experience life?

- Why do women think differently, act differently and feel differently about situations and life circumstances than men?

- Some of the authors cite God as a strong influence in their life experiences. Do you think it makes a difference if a woman has a religious background or not, as to how she views life or handles difficult situations? Why or why not?

- What did you personally learn from this book?

- If this book were written by males instead of females, how would that change the book? What would you use as the title?

About the Authors

Stacey Schneider is a freelance writer and journal editor, as well as a professor at Northeast Ohio Medical University in Rootstown, Ohio. She earned her Doctor of Pharmacy degree and practiced as a pharmacist for many years in the community but teaching and writing emerged as her true life calling. Writing began for her as a means to heal her own scars and has since transformed into one of her true passions. It's not unusual to find Stacey sitting at her antique desk engrossed in reading a great book or writing amidst the peacefulness. Stacey hopes to share her own experiences to empower other women to see the light at the end of the tunnel and realize we must all take our own journeys to find and embrace our true selves. In her spare time, you will find her enjoying running to clear her mind, spending time with family, and relishing in the tranquil serenity of the koi fishpond in her backyard.

Thinking outside of the box ... that's what *Lori Bodkin* does best! You might say creativity is her middle name and it certainly keeps her passion for life in overdrive. Lori lives in St. Clairsville, Ohio and has been married to her husband Bob for sixteen years. Together, they enjoy spending time with their son and daughter. "Make a difference everyday" is Lori's personal mission statement, and it is evident in her daily activities. Lori has coordinated and led many leadership workshops, fun-themed retreats, Bible studies and women's events for various organizations where she has enjoyed being a mentor and a motivational speaker. Lori has a bachelor's degree in Accounting, is a certified Christian Lay Counselor and also writes an encouragement blog called *Arrows of Integrity*. With active children, free time always comes at a premium, but when it's available, Lori enjoys scrapbooking, reading, baking, and especially visiting with her girlfriends over a cup of good coffee.

www.ingramcontent.com/pod-product-compliance
Lightning Source LLC
Chambersburg PA
CBHW051345040426
42453CB00007B/415